Hereditary

A24

He's facing forward in the driver's seat, completely frozen. He can't bear to look back. In the back seat is his sister Charlie's BODY, covered in thick, tar-like blood. Only the body. No head. If he looks up ever so slightly, he will be able to see her through the rearview mirror. So he can't even move his eyes. Eventually, he gets out of the car without looking at all. Once dawn breaks, he will hear his mother's scream.

Even more terrifying than the decapitated girl in the back seat is the fact that we, as an audience, may have — subconsciously — hoped for Charlie's death. Of course this is not the film's "official" stance — to root for a child's death. But when Charlie makes annoying sounds with her tongue, or when she cuts the head off a dead pigeon, the movie is undoubtedly sending signals that fill us with sinister thoughts.

While the film is an impeccable work of genre in which occult elements are cleverly, tightly woven together, I wonder if genre is just a cover for the real horror. Because the true horror comes from the family itself. One of the most terrifying scenes in the film is the dimly lit dinner scene, which has no occult elements and relies solely on Toni Collette's explosive performance.The film is ostensibly about the hell that a family suffers as generation after generation is swallowed by a demon, but it's actually saying that family itself (or ties defined by blood) is hell.

In *Hereditary*, Ari Aster goes beyond the trappings of genre and delivers true, profound horror. A horror that is primal and inescapable. In order to survive this overwhelming horror, we cast a spell on ourselves. We hope that the gruesome moments we witnessed will eventually settle into a "neutral view of the accident," like an innocuous tableau made up of adorable miniature figures.

BONG JOON HO

SECTION I

HEREDITARY

BY ARI ASTER

INT. WORKSHOP – MORNING

Through glass: a very large TREEHOUSE. It is joined to a sturdy oak and hovers fifteen feet above the ground. We PULL BACK from the glass to reveal the frame of a window, and as we PAN away from this window, we reveal that we are in...

An impressive room serving as an ARTIST'S WORKSHOP. It's empty, but evidence of frantic creative activity abounds.

We PAN across the wall, crossing a series of meticulously hand-crafted DOLLHOUSES, mostly works in progress. As we drift past these unfinished dioramas, our trajectory becomes clearer...

We are moving in on an extraordinary sculpture of a beautiful, rustic CRAFTSMAN HOME, at 1:8 scale. Its front wall has been removed, exposing its rooms in graphic tableaux. This huge miniature is pain-stakingly detailed. It's adorned with shrunken props/decorations (flashlights, pill bottles, shoes, etc.) and teensy furniture, all flawlessly rendered and distinguishable ONLY IN SIZE from their full-scale models.

We continue to pan/track across the miniature, edging CLOSER AND CLOSER as we drift along its tiny rooms. We finally arrive at a miniature replica of a TEENAGE BOY'S BEDROOM on the second floor.

We push toward this until the ROOM FILLS THE FRAME. The bright morning sun beams in through its window. It becomes apparent that a handsome, skinny BOY is sleeping in the bed. This is PETER GRAHAM (17).

We continue pushing gently in, remaining in a wide of the room (whose status as a miniature has now been confused). The door opens and STEVE GRAHAM (47) — tall, broad-shouldered, formal — pops his head in. He wears a black suit.

STEVE

All right, Petey. Wake up time.

Peter stirs awake. Steve drops a folded-up BLACK SUIT AND TIE on the foot of the bed.

STEVE (CONT'D)

Here's your suit.

MAX, the family's golden retriever, shuffles happily in through the door.

EXT. GRAHAM HOUSE - SAME TIME

12 Wide on the house, revealing that it is IDENTICAL to the miniature that we saw in the workshop.

Steve exits a back door to approach the TREEHOUSE from the opening. We are subtly BOOMING DOWN from this wide view (as Steve arrives at the tree and proceeds to climb) to settle on a parked CAR — one of two family cars — in the foreground.

Sitting in the passenger seat is a bereaved woman (45). She wears all black and is beautiful in a worn way. This is ANNIE GRAHAM, and she looks emotionally exhausted.

She leans forward to pick up a little wooden jewelry box (floral text on the top reads "*Mommy loves Annie*"). Annie opens it to pull out a delicate NECKLACE bearing an ORNATE SIGIL. She holds it up. Scrutinizes it.

INT. TREEHOUSE - SAME TIME

Steve pokes his head into the treehouse, where he finds:

CHARLIE — a plump, androgynous thirteen-year-old girl — lying asleep on the floor. She wears a hoodie and pajama bottoms. Beside her is a DRAWING PAD and an open SHOEBOX.

STEVE

Charlie, are you crazy?!

Charlie wakes up, her nose pink and runny. When she notices Steve, she frantically reaches to SHUT the shoebox.

STEVE (CONT'D)

What are you doing? It was freezing last night. This is how you get pneumonia!

CHARLIE

(getting up)

It's okay.

STEVE

(already climbing back down)

Your mom's in the car already, we're *late*.

INT. FUNERAL HOME - CHAPEL - MORNING

A moderately attended FUNERAL. (A large group of MEN AND WOMEN observe from the back.)

Before the altar, an OPEN CASKET rests beside a blown-up photo
13 of the deceased ELLEN LEIGH, Annie's 75-year-old mother.

Annie, Steve, Charlie (now wearing an oversized black dress over her pajama bottoms), and Peter sit in the first row of chairs. They listen as a LARGE WOMAN (60s) speaks in remembrance of Ellen.

LARGE WOMAN

Ellen was a tough one. She didn't mince words — at all! She was NOT sentimental. But she was honest. And I know that's how she raised her children, Annie and Charles —

(uncomfortably)

— may he rest in peace... To always be honest...

Half-listening (half-wincing), Annie's attention is drawn to CHARLIE, who makes a quiet CLICKING noise with her tongue. *This is a tic.*

Suddenly, a bird FLAPS out from the rafters, startling the congregation.

The bird settles on a ceiling perch. It is a WHIPPOORWILL. It looks down, fixing its gaze on Annie. Annie looks very disturbed. Off-screen, the large woman continues.

MINUTES LATER

Annie is now on the PLATFORM.

ANNIE

It's heartening to see so many strange new faces here today. I know my mom would be very touched (and probably a little suspicious, ha) if she could see this turnout, so...

Annie looks down to now read from a heavily edited loose-leaf page. This is her eulogy. (Not used to reading in public, she rarely looks up from the paper.)

ANNIE (CONT'D)

My mother was a very secretive and private woman. She had private rituals, private friends, private anxieties... It honestly feels like a betrayal just to be standing here talking about her...

Annie pauses. She looks at the paragraph. It's very long, and begins with the sentence *"My mother was a chameleon."* She decides to skip ahead to the next paragraph.

ANNIE (CONT'D)

She was a very difficult woman to read. If you ever thought you knew what was going on with her — and God forbid you tried to confront that...!

(stops...pauses...skips ahead)

ANNIE (CONT'D)

... But when her life was unpolluted, she could be the sweetest, warmest, most loving person in the world...

Charlie is DRAWING a weepy caricature of Annie at the platform. Steve watches this in the corner of his eye.

ANNIE (CONT'D)

(pauses, skips again to the next paragraph)

... She was also incredibly stubborn. Which I'm sure explains me. You could always count on her to always have the answer...

She stops short, eyes on the paper. The sentence would continue *"and if she ever WAS mistaken, that was YOUR opinion and you were WRONG."*

Suddenly remorseful, Annie looks up. Now off-book, she awkwardly asserts:

ANNIE (CONT'D)
I did love her.

Charlie is still drawing. Steve closes the notepad. He points to Annie: *"Listen to your mother."* Charlie grudgingly obliges.

ANNIE (CONT'D)
She was especially strong about food. When I was a girl and I had to eat my veggies...

INT. FUNERAL HOME – VIEWING ROOM – LATER

The mourners have formed a queue to view the deceased. First in line are Annie, Steve, and Peter (who doesn't look). They each shuffle past the OPEN CASKET.

Charlie's turn. She peers into the casket to see her grandmother's CORPSE. It wears a NECKLACE with a delicate SIGIL ORNAMENT (identical to Annie's). The seams in the corpse's makeup are eerily apparent and the lips are slightly twisted.

15 Unnerved, Charlie looks away. She meets eyes with a smiling MIDDLE-AGED BLONDE MAN standing in the queue behind her. He's STARING at her — an overly sentimental look in his eyes.

Disturbed, Charlie averts her eyes. *"Yeesh."* She walks off with a click of the tongue. She draws a CHOCOLATE BAR out of her pocket.

Before leaving the room, Charlie stops by the door. She looks back to see...

CHARLIE'S POV: A gaunt WOMAN has arrived at the open casket. Her finger is dipped into a small bottle of OIL. She quickly and covertly STREAKS the oil along the corpse's lips. *(A following mourner, seeing this, squints with bewilderment.)*

Charlie doesn't react to this. Eyes still on the casket, she unwraps her candy, but is startled when —

STEVE appears, resting his hand on her shoulder. Charlie TENSES UP as Steve gently guides her out of the room.

STEVE
(re: candy bar)
There aren't nuts in that, are there?

CHARLIE

(very irritated)

No.

Annie joins them.

ANNIE

Are there nuts in that?

STEVE

No.

ANNIE (CONT'D)

Because we don't have the Epipen.

EXT. GRAHAM HOUSE – LATE AFTERNOON

The car parks in front of the house. Everyone climbs out to approach the house.

CHARLIE

(quietly)

I don't like being back without grandma.

ANNIE

(carefully)

Well, sweetie... do you understand why we have to?

INT. GRAHAM HOUSE – FOYER – CONTINUOUS

The house is unlit and seemingly vacant.

Off-screen, we hear FEET SCURRYING and a DOOR CLOSING. Max, the golden retriever, BARKS in reaction to this.

A moment later, the front door opens and the Graham family enters.

Max runs up, desperate to greet them. Steve bends down to happily receive him.

Charlie moves toward the stairs, still wearing her shoes.

STEVE

Hey hey — shoes off.

Charlie comes back down to pull off her shoes. She'll then go straight upstairs.

ANNIE
(suddenly self-conscious)
Should I be sadder?

STEVE
You should feel however you feel.

Steve, now looking down, notices dried FOOTPRINTS around the foyer.

STEVE (CONT'D)
(calling out)
Okay, see?! What's with all these footprints? I'm tired of reminding everybody.

INT. WORKSHOP - EVENING

Annie is at her work desk. It's a mess of paints, props, wood pieces, etc. She wears magnifying eye-glasses as she carefully paints eyes onto a SMALL DOCTOR FIGURINE for a MINIATURE HOSPICE. A figurine of an old woman — presumably Annie's mother — lies in a miniature hospital bed.

Steve enters, disrupting Annie's focus.

STEVE
How's it going?

ANNIE
Just working.

Steve casually rests a glass of water and a PILL on the table. She downs it without question.

STEVE
Still toiling on the hospice?

ANNIE
Between that and the pre-school.

There is a half-finished MINIATURE PRE-SCHOOL in the corner.

STEVE
How far are we now? Seven months?

ANNIE
Six and a half.

STEVE

Yow. Comin' up.

Her eyes widen with stress.

STEVE (CONT'D)

Any title ideas yet?

Annie grabs her laptop and pulls up a PDF for a poster promoting an upcoming EXHIBITION of her artwork. It features a photo of a magnificent living room miniature. Below this are the words "TITLE HERE" in bold, followed by *"The Work of Annie Leigh."*

ANNIE

This is the photo they wanna use.

STEVE (CONT'D)

Ooh, I love that one.

ANNIE (CONT'D)

The gallery owner keeps suggesting *Your Life in Miniature* for the collection.

STEVE

What do *you* think of that?

Annie looks at him, incredulous. *"Are you serious?"*

STEVE (CONT'D)

(conceding)

Okay. Yeah. A little trite.

ANNIE

Are you kidding?! She won't stop pushing it!

Steve looks to a stack of LARGE MOVING BOXES in the corner. They're marked *"Mom's Things"* in Annie's handwriting.

STEVE

(running his hands through her hair)

You want me to put that stuff in the attic?

ANNIE

... Yeah. Maybe not just yet.

INT. PETER'S BEDROOM - NIGHT

Peter sits up in bed, holding a guitar. He improvises a clunky tune as a muted TV plays cartoons. His eyes are on the TV.

The door cracks open and Steve pokes his head in.

STEVE
Goodnight, kiddo.

PETER
'Night, Dad.

STEVE
... What you playing?

PETER
Just plucking random strings.

STEVE
(nods, then)
You feeling okay about everything?

PETER
(shrugs)
Yeah. Fine.

STEVE
Little sad?

19

Peter shrugs again. He clearly wasn't fond of Ellen.

STEVE (CONT'D)
Yeah. I know.
(pause)
Okay, buddy. Love you.

Steve KISSES in Peter's direction. Peter kisses back. Steve walks off, leaving the door open.

A moment later, Annie walks up to the doorway, still wearing her magnifying eye-glasses. She's holding a prop in one hand, a fine paint-brush in the other.

ANNIE
'Night sweetheart.

PETER
Goodnight. I'm sorry about your mom.

ANNIE
(pause)
Thank you. I'm sorry about your grandma.

PETER

... Thank you.

Annie smiles, hesitates, and walks off. There's a very loaded tension between these two.

After Annie is gone, Peter climbs out of bed to shut the door. He LOCKS it.

INT. CHARLIE'S BEDROOM – NIGHT

Charlie's room is that of a young artist. The walls are covered in drawings, and the desks and other surfaces are littered with different HANDMADE HUMAN MANIKINS and SMALL STATUES (all made of disparate parts — mostly found objects).

Annie sits on the edge of Charlie's bed. Charlie is under the covers. Annie has opened Charlie's drawing pad to see a CARICATURE of Annie's mother's corpse in its casket.

ANNIE

That's grandma?

CHARLIE

I dunno.

ANNIE

You know you were her favorite.

CHARLIE

(looking away)

No I wasn't.

ANNIE

(pouncing)

Oh yes you *absolutely* were! Even when you were a little baby, she wouldn't let me *feed* you because she needed to feed you. It drove me *crazy.*

CHARLIE

She said I was supposed to be a boy.

Annie knows this. She hesitates, wanting to say the right thing.

ANNIE

How do *you* feel about that?

Charlie shrugs.

ANNIE (CONT'D)
You know, *I* was a tomboy growing up. I *hated* dresses and dolls and *pink*.

Charlie's heard this before. She has tensed up.

CHARLIE
(looking away, quietly)
Who's gonna take care of me?

ANNIE
(mock offended)
Ummm, excuse me? You don't think *I'm* gonna take care of you?!

CHARLIE
But when *you* die...

ANNIE
... Then *Dad* would take care of you. Or Peter.

Charlie's head remains turned. Discouraged, Annie turns back the page of the drawing pad. She now sees the caricature of *her*, crying at the pulpit.

21

ANNIE (CONT'D)
Who's this one?

No answer. Annie takes it personally, but pretends not to. She closes the book with a smile.

ANNIE (CONT'D)
You never even cried as a baby — you know that? Not even when you were born.

Charlie ignores this.

ANNIE (CONT'D)
Did you feel like you wanted to cry *today?*

Without looking at Annie, Charlie shrugs a tense "I don't know."

ANNIE (CONT'D)
Do you think that might feel like a relief?

Charlie remains miles away.

Annie looks up to notice that a difficult-to-read WORD (looks like *"Satony"*) has been CARVED into the wall behind

Charlie's bed. Annie pauses, lets it go, and then bends down to KISS Charlie's forehead.

ANNIE (CONT'D)
Goodnight, sweetie.

INT. WORKSHOP – NIGHT

Annie enters. Outside the window: trees rustling.

Annie hesitates before walking over to the box labeled *"Mom's Things."* She reluctantly opens it...

The box is filled with bottled oils and herbs. At the top of the box is a PHOTO ALBUM titled *"Memories."* Annie opens it to sift through photos of her mother. She lays the album back into the box, and then notices a stack of worn HARDBACKS. She pulls one out. *"NOTES ON SPIRITUALISM."*

This calls back unwelcome memories. Annie dumps the book back into the box, and PUSHES the box away.

Annie walks to the door and flips off the light, leaving the room in darkness (save for the moonlight). She's about to leave, but something makes her FREEZE.

Standing motionless in a dark corner (almost too dark to make out) is ANNIE'S MOTHER, ELLEN — wearing the same outfit as she was at the funeral. She's staring at Annie. SMILING.

Annie, nearly paralyzed with fear, reaches for the light switch. Without looking away, she turns the light back ON.

Her mother is gone.

Annie remains motionless.

ANNIE
(a whisper)
Mom?

Annie's eyes are now drawn to...

A dusty older MINIATURE in the corner. It's a replica of Annie's bedroom. A figurine of Annie (in her early thirties) BREASTFEEDS a baby. Standing beside her is a figurine of an OLDER WOMAN (Annie's mother) holding her naked BREAST out of her nightgown. She leans over, offering it to the baby. *Competing with Annie.*

Troubled by this, Annie walks briskly to the miniature and TURNS it away. It's now facing the wall as Annie returns to the door, flicks off the light, and leaves.

INT. ANNIE & STEVE'S BEDROOM – MINUTES LATER

Annie climbs into bed with Steve.

ANNIE
I just scared myself in the workshop.

STEVE
Oh no. With what?

Annie pauses. Thinks about telling him. Steve looks interested / slightly worried. Annie thinks better of it.

STEVE (CONT'D)
. . . No?

She smiles *"nah."*

ANNIE
Goodnight.

23

Annie turns off the bedside lamp and gives Steve a blunt kiss.

STEVE
(before she can pull away)
Mm-mm — no you don't.

He EXTENDS the kiss, making it last. Then:

STEVE (CONT'D)
Goodnight.

INT. HIGH SCHOOL CLASSROOM – NEXT MORNING

Charlie's "special needs" class.

Scrawled on the blackboard are the words *"Quiet means Silence!"* and all the students are indeed silent as they take a quiz.

The TEACHER (40s) walks along the rows of desks, overlooking the quiz-takers. He comes to CHARLIE, whose quiz is upside down. In her lap, she is assembling a small manikin's body with disparate found objects (wood, plastic, cardboard, etc).

TEACHER

Are you done?

CHARLIE

(looking up, startled)

What?

(then)

... Almost.

TEACHER

(warmly)

So maybe we finish the toy *after* the quiz? What do you think?

CHARLIE

... Okay.

The teacher gently turns the quiz right-side up. Charlie is extremely tense through this.

Suddenly a PIGEON flies into the window, slamming its head. The impact breaks its neck.

The classroom erupts with excitement — *"Oh my God!" "Did you see that?!"* — but not Charlie. She stares tensely at her desk, still disturbed by the teacher's interference.

Charlie's EYES scan up. They alight on a pair of SCISSORS on the teacher's desk.

INT. HIGH SCHOOL CLASSROOM – DAY

Peter's English class. The chalkboard reads:

<u>Themes</u>
- Escaping Fate.
- Relationship between knowledge and responsibility.
- "No man considered fortunate until he is dead."

The teacher, MR. DAVIES (30s), tries to facilitate a group discussion. He holds a copy of Sophocles' *The Women of Trachis.*

MR. DAVIES

So if we're going by the rule that a hero is undone by his fatal flaw, what was Heracles' flaw?

SMART-ASS STUDENT

Fucking his mom.

Laughter from a couple stoners.

MR. DAVIES
Wrong play, Sam. And that's two strikes now.

Meanwhile, Peter is being hypnotized by BRIDGET (17), the attractive girl sitting in front of him. Peter's rapt attention is glued to the butt of her jeans.

MR. DAVIES (CONT'D)
Come on, guys: what was *Heracles'* flaw?

Bridget now speaks up:

BRIDGET
Arrogance.

This piques Peter's interest.

MR. DAVIES
Okay — why?

BRIDGET
Because he literally *refuses* to look at all the signs that are being literally *handed* to him the *entire* play.

Peter's in love.

MR. DAVIES
Okay, interesting! So he thinks he has control. But also, don't forget: Sophocles writes it so the oracle is unconditional. Meaning Heracles never *had* any choice. Right?

Peter's smartphone VIBRATES with a text.

MR. DAVIES (CONT'D)
So, does this make it more tragic or less tragic than if he *did* have a choice?

STUDENT #2
Less!

Peter checks his text. It's from Brendan. It reads: *"Wanna smoke a bowl at break?"* This came from the BOY behind him.

MR. DAVIES
Okay: why?

STUDENT #2

(already giving up)

Because!

Mr. Davies turns to Peter, who's now composing a text in his lap.

MR. DAVIES

Care to weigh in, Peter?

Peter looks up, a deer in headlights.

PETER

About which part?

MR. DAVIES

Is it more tragic if it's inevitable than if the characters had agency?

Peter is not following.

PETER

Yes?

MR. DAVIES

Why?

Peter has nothing. Another student picks up the slack:

STUDENT #3

I think it's *more* tragic — because if it's all just *inevitable*, that means the characters have no hope and that they *never* had hope, because they're just like *pawns* in this horrible, hopeless *machine*.

Peter has now noticed BRIDGET looking at him. She gives him a sardonic *"nice try"* smile. Peter smiles back, embarrassed. She turns away. Peter's smile turns to a longing stare.

EXT. SCHOOLYARD – DAY

Recess.

The DEAD PIGEON lies pathetically in the bushes below Charlie's classroom window.

Charlie stands nearby, staring at the pigeon. After some time, she fishes a pair of SCISSORS from her parka pocket. (These are the scissors from her teacher's desk.)

Charlie extends the scissors, fits the blades around the pigeon's neck, and SNIPS OFF ITS HEAD.

Charlie quickly POCKETS the pigeon head, and looks up to notice:

An OLDER WOMAN (60s) sitting on a bench, just beyond the schoolyard fence. She is gazing at Charlie, sentimental.

Charlie gawks at the woman, unnerved. Without breaking eye contact, she pulls a chocolate bar from her pocket and takes a bite.

INT. PSYCHIATRIST'S OFFICE – AFTERNOON

Steve's office is large and sparsely decorated.

Steve sits in a leather chair with a notepad resting on his lap. Sitting opposite him is an extremely agitated, depressed female PATIENT (40s). Steve studies her non-judgmentally.

STEVE
And how's the anger?

PATIENT
Same. I just don't care as much.

STEVE
Not as consuming maybe?

PATIENT
(gritted teeth)
It's just as *consuming*, I just don't *care* as much.

Steve, nods.

STEVE
And still the same trouble sleeping?

Her eyes widen an annoyed "yes."

STEVE (CONT'D)
How about drinking?

PATIENT
You said I should stop.

STEVE
Did you?

PATIENT
You said I *had* to! With the Sarafem.

STEVE
Okay, thank you, I'm glad...! And how's *that* been? Versus the Lexapro.

The woman tries to summon the energy to answer him. Steve continues to affect superhuman patience.

INT. ANNIE'S WORKSHOP – DAY

Annie's laptop is open to an amateur blog: *"Notes Toward the Discernment of Apparitions."*

Annie, sitting at the Graham house model, is carefully painting a MINIATURE LAPTOP featuring the very same website.

INT. ANNIE'S MOTHER'S BEDROOM – DAY

We are looking through the open door into the HALL.

Downstairs, the front door is heard opening.

STEVE (O.S.)
Hello!

ANNIE (O.S.)
Hi!

Annie steps out into the hall and walks past the doorway. A moment later, we hear her footsteps FREEZE. She soon returns into view, now looking very unsettled. She stares *past* us, into the room...

ANNIE'S POV: The room is mostly EMPTY, save for the bed (stripped of sheets), a bookshelf, and various FRAMED PHOTOS featuring members of the family. One photo: a portrait of Annie and her mother, standing side by side. There is also a LARGE TRIANGLE (pointed northwest) that has been CARVED violently into the floorboards.

Annie doesn't react to the triangle. It was clearly already there.

Annie leaves.

INT. TV ROOM – MOMENTS LATER

Steve sits on the couch, having just turned on the news. He's still wearing his coat.

Annie enters.

ANNIE
Were you in my mom's room?

STEVE
What? No.

ANNIE
The door was open.

Steve makes a *"hmm"* face.

The front door is heard opening, and Annie goes to the FOYER, where Peter and Charlie are entering.

ANNIE (CONT'D)
Hey, guys. How was school?

PETER
Okay.

ANNIE
Did either of you go into Grandma's room
29 recently?

They both squint. *"Why would we EVER go in there?"*

INT. HALLWAY - EVENING

Steve is at Annie's mother's door. He LOCKS IT (by key) from the outside.

ANNIE
Sorry. I know it's irrational.

STEVE
Not at all.

Illustrating that it's locked, Steve tries turning the knob. Annie smiles.

ANNIE
Thank you.

She kisses Steve, feeling dopey.

Peter walks up to them, holding the PHONE.

PETER

Dad?

(extending phone)

It's the cemetery.

ANNIE

About what?

STEVE

(accepting the phone)

I'll see.

Steve starts to move away.

STEVE (CONT'D)

(into phone)

Hi… Yeah…

Steve walks down the hall to create distance between him and Annie. Now irked, Annie walks off.

STEVE (CONT'D)

(into phone, warily)

Okay… And what does "desecrated" mean?

(listens, then — shocked)

What? It's only been a *week*.

ANNIE steps back into the hall, now wearing a coat. Steve nervously accelerates:

STEVE (CONT'D)

(into phone)

Okay. All right. Can I actually call you back?…
Okay, fine.

Steve hangs up.

ANNIE

What was it?

STEVE

Nothing. Just billing crap.

Annie looks skeptical.

Steve notices Annie's COAT. He gives her an inquiring look.

ANNIE

I'm gonna go see a movie.

STEVE

Okay. Right now?

ANNIE

I think I just need to get out of the house for a second.

STEVE

... Want me to join?

ANNIE

(hesitates)

I think I might just need like an hour to myself. I'm really tense.

STEVE

Okay... great. I think you should.

Annie smiles *"thanks."*

ANNIE

Do you know where Charlie is?

STEVE

31 Where *else?*

Annie knows what that means. She immediately looks frustrated.

STEVE (CONT'D)

Let it go. It's wasted energy.

ANNIE

It's freezing outside!

STEVE (CONT'D)

So let her catch a cold. Maybe she needs one.

INT. TREEHOUSE – EVENING

Charlie sits in her treehouse. She lays the severed pigeon head in her SHOEBOX. Inside this box are three other SEVERED ANIMAL HEADS. One belongs to a rabbit, one to a rat, one to a squirrel. (The heads are in different stages of decomposition; flies buzz about.)

Down below, Annie is heard:

ANNIE (O.S.)

Charlie?

Charlie shuts the box, SHOVES it into a corner, and peers down to see ANNIE at the tree's base.

ANNIE (CONT'D)
Come on, sweetie. It's freezing out here.

No response from Charlie. Annie doesn't push it.

ANNIE (CONT'D)
Okay, well, I'm running out for a sec. Is there anything I can bring you back?

CHARLIE
(defensively)
Why??

INT. CAR (MOVING) - NIGHT

Annie idles into the parking lot of a Catholic high school.

She parks, turns off the engine, and sits in silence for a moment. Bracing herself.

INT. CATHOLIC SCHOOL GYMNASIUM - NIGHT

A SUPPORT GROUP held in the high school's gymnasium. A sign on an easel reads *"LOSING A LOVED ONE, Grief Recovery."* The session hasn't yet started. Twenty empty chairs form a CIRCLE in the space's center.

Mourners of varying affect are scattered about, mingling.

Annie ENTERS, very ill at ease.

THIRTY MINUTES LATER

All the chairs are now filled. A middle-aged MEXICAN WOMAN speaks (in Spanish) through coursing tears. A YOUNG MAN translates for her as the rest of the group listens.

YOUNG MAN
(translating between her sentences)
Sometimes I feel guilty because I feel so relieved... Because he was in so much pain, and by the end he just hated himself. Always saying "I'm a burden, I'm a burden, I'm a burden"...

Annie's eyes are wide. She's empathizing with this, but it seems to also be agitating her.

FIVE MINUTES LATER

The GROUP LEADER addresses the group.

LEADER

We've set aside some time for any newcomers
who might like to speak...

Silence.

LEADER (CONT'D)

So, anybody new — if it's your first or second time
with us: the floor is open.

Annie looks very torn. She starts to lift up her hand, but stops short.

LEADER (CONT'D)

(gesturing to Annie)

Yes?

Annie looks panicked.

LEADER (CONT'D)

Would you like to...?

33

ANNIE

... Maybe not.

LEADER

Okay. No pressure.

Annie nods, wavers, and then forces herself:

ANNIE

My name's Annie.

THE GROUP

Hi, Annie.

Annie strains a smile. She continues tensely, as if against her will:

ANNIE

My mom died a week ago, so I'm just here for —
trying it. I have a lot of resistance to things like
this, but I went to these a couple years ago —
I was pressured to come — but it *did* help, so...

(MORE)

(long pause)
My mom was old and she wasn't all together at the end — and we were pretty much *estranged* before that — so it wasn't a huge blow. But I *did* love her. And she didn't have an easy life... She had D.I.D., which became extreme in the last year, and *dementia...!* My dad died of starvation when I was a baby. He had psychotic depression and he starved himself. Which I'm sure was as pleasant as it sounds. And then my *older* brother — he was schizophrenic — and when *he* was sixteen, he hanged himself in my mom's bedroom. Of course his suicide note blamed *her*. Accusing her of putting *people* inside of him.
(throws hands up)
So that was my *mom's* life!

Annie looks to the group. They allow her time to continue. She reluctantly proceeds.

ANNIE (CONT'D)
... She finally lived in our house at the end. Before hospice. We weren't talking before that — or we *were* and then we *weren't* and then we *were* — she was *completely* manipulative — until finally my husband enforced a No Contact rule, which lasted until I was pregnant with my daughter. I didn't let her *near* me when I had my first — my son — which is <u>why</u> I gave her my daughter, who she *immediately* stabbed her hooks into. And of course I felt guilty *again* when she got sick... Not that she was even my *mom* at the end. And not that she *ever* felt guilty. About *anything*.

Annie has worked herself up. A charged pause as she calms back down.

ANNIE (CONT'D)
And I don't wanna put any *more* stress on my family. Not even sure if they <u>could</u> give me that support.

She gets stuck here. Tears begin to well. She struggles to squeeze out the following:

ANNIE (CONT'D)
It just all sometimes feels ruined. And then I realize *I'm* to blame. Or not that I'm <u>to</u> blame, but that I'm... *blamed*.

Beat.

LEADER

And what do you think you feel blamed for?

Annie looks to the leader. Pauses.

ANNIE

I don't know...! I apparently acted a certain way? According to them. In my sleep. A couple years ago...

Annie looks like she's going to continue, but then she abruptly cuts herself off. That's it.

We reveal the mystified GROUP. They struggle to remain sympathetic, despite their confusion.

ANNIE (CONT'D)

So anyway. Everything's disappointing. So here I am.

She forces a laugh, but also cries a bit. She wipes away the tears and makes an embarrassed *"bah"* face. She then motions to the group:
35 *"Who's next?"*

INT. HALLWAY - NIGHT

At the end of the hall, a very depleted Annie has just finished scaling the stairs.

In the f.g., Peter's door eases shut.

INT. PETER'S BEDROOM - CONTINUOUS

Peter's laptop is open. The browser displays BRIDGET'S FACEBOOK PAGE. (Peter has been going through her photos.) Behind that, another page displays *"POPULAR CAREER INTERESTS."*

Peter walks from the door (which he just closed) to his desk. He grabs a small water pipe, packed with marijuana, and walks to the window.

As Peter takes a hit from his pipe, his smartphone vibrates with a TEXT. He checks it.

From *Brendan:*

Holy shit. Huge party tomorrow at Aaron's house. Bring your dick!

EXT. GRAHAM HOUSE – CONTINUOUS

A WIDE of the house. In the foreground seems to be someone's SHOULDER.

Pot smoke is blown out of Peter's window.

INT. CHARLIE'S BEDROOM – THE NEXT DAY

Charlie, dressed in her pajamas and munching on M&Ms, sits at her desk. She is finishing the torso for another small human manikin. The limbs are made of different scraps.

To the side of Charlie's sculpture-in-progress is the SEVERED PIGEON HEAD. Beside *that* is Charlie's drawing pad, open to an unfinished STILL LIFE of the pigeon head. And on the *far* side of the desk: a crude, bare stage for an unfinished DIORAMA.

As she works, Charlie makes the CLICKING SOUND with her tongue.

Suddenly, a GLINT of light sweeps the room in a quick FLASH.

Charlie ceases drawing. Her clicking STOPS. Disturbed by the flash, she raises her head and HOLDS. Listening for something?

After a beat, Charlie rises from her seat and walks to the WINDOW. She stands there for a long time, her back to us. She's STARING at something...

INT. KITCHEN – SAME TIME

Annie is preparing dinner. Her smartphone DINGS with an INCOMING EMAIL. It's from *The Asher Gallery*. She opens it. It reads:

> *Hi Annie!*
>
> *Don't want to bother you, but we'd love to see where we are (progress-wise). Could you possibly send us pics of your work in its current stage? I promise we won't judge!! ;)*

Annie looks suddenly overwhelmed.

EXT. WOODS – MINUTES LATER

The vast WOODED AREA behind the Graham house. It clearly rained earlier.

Charlie, wearing only socks and still dressed in her pajamas, takes wide steps as she slogs through the mud.

She gazes listlessly ahead, as if in a TRANCE. She's being drawn toward something. As if she's sleepwalking with open eyes.

Max, the family dog, follows happily behind. A FIRE is heard crackling in the distance. *Is this what she's walking toward?*

We cut to an EXTREME HIGH ANGLE — almost bird's-eye. This reveals that Charlie seems to be following a FRESH PATH OF FOOTPRINTS (source unknown) leading off-screen.

INT. ANNIE'S WORKSHOP – SAME TIME

Annie is now WORKING INTENSELY on one of her miniatures. She looks very anxious.

Peter appears at the door.

PETER

Hey, uh…

Annie looks up, visibly annoyed by the disturbance.

PETER (CONT'D)

… Do you think I could borrow one of the cars tonight?

ANNIE

Why? Where are you going?

PETER

Oh, just like a school BBQ thing.

Annie continues working on the miniature, breaking intermittently as they speak:

ANNIE

Does that mean you're not having dinner with us?

PETER

Oh, no, I was still gonna eat here.

ANNIE

Well — you can eat *there* if you want. I just didn't realize.

PETER (CONT'D)

No, I'll eat here. I'd just be going there to hang out.

Annie pauses. Her mind is not quite on this right now. She takes a moment (pulling herself from her work) to assess the questions that need to be asked.

ANNIE

No drinking?

PETER

Nobody's old enough to even *get* drinks if they wanted to.

ANNIE

Well, *that's a crock*. I'm just asking if *you're* drinking.

PETER

Well, I just answered no.

Annie looks him hard in the eye before accepting that.

ANNIE

… You gonna take your sister?

PETER

Uh — does she want to go?

ANNIE

(mimicking his tone)

Uh — have you asked her?

EXT. HALLWAY – MOMENTS LATER

Peter goes to Charlie's room. She's not there. He calls out:

PETER

Charlie?!

INT. WORKSHOP – MOMENTS LATER

Peter returns to the workshop.

PETER

She's not in the house.

Frustrated, Annie throws down her paintbrush:

ANNIE

What? Yes she is.

EXT. WOODS - SAME TIME

Charlie is still walking through the mud. She sees in the DISTANCE, *almost too far away to distinguish...*

A ring of BURNING TORCHES has been set up. Within this ring, an OLD WOMAN'S INANIMATE BODY (dead?) stands erect — tied to a pole, with her arms strapped to outstretched planks.
The body is dressed in FINE WHITE SILK. It looks like Ellen Leigh (Charlie's grandmother), but it's too far away to *quite* tell.

Charlie squints at this, barely reacting, when —

ANNIE (O.S.)
CHARLIE!

Charlie looks to ANNIE, who is running in her direction.

Charlie steps toward Annie.

ANNIE (CONT'D)
What are you *doing?!* You leave the house barefoot?

39 Annie arrives at Charlie, *not seeing the distant torches.* She seizes Charlie's arm and starts leading her back to the house.

ANNIE (CONT'D)
Are you an *idiot?* You can't just roam around — no shoes, no coat!

Charlie YANKS her arm away from Annie.

ANNIE (CONT'D)
Oh — what? You're *angry* with me?

Annie GRABS Charlie's arm and PULLS her back toward the house.

CHARLIE
(under her breath)
I want Grandma.

ANNIE
Yeah. That makes *one* of us.

INT. FOYER - MOMENTS LATER

Annie and Charlie return. Annie stamps/scrapes the mud off her shoes.

ANNIE
You're going to this party with your brother.

CHARLIE
What party?

ANNIE
(trying to be softer)
A school hangout with other kids.

CHARLIE
(evasive)
That's okay.

ANNIE
No, it's *not* okay. You're going.

CHARLIE
Why?

ANNIE
Because it'll be *fun*. You can hang *out*.

CHARLIE
With *who?*

ANNIE (CONT'D)
With your *brother!* With other *kids!*

Peter has stepped into the hall. He nods, as if to say *"yeah, come along,"* but his eyes are very uninviting.

CHARLIE
(as if to challenge Peter)
... Fine.

ANNIE
Great. You're going.
(to Peter)
She's going with you.

PETER
Great.

ANNIE
And that *really* means no drinking.

PETER
Yeah: I *really* wasn't going to.

EXT. HIGHWAY – EVENING

The sun has set. A FULL MOON glows pale-blue over a lonely highway.

The Graham family car (the green one) FLASHES past.

INT. GRAHAM FAMILY CAR – CONTINUOUS

Peter is tense at the wheel. He drives the speed limit.

Peter's eyes drift to the REAR VIEW MIRROR… Charlie, sitting in the back, CLICKS her tongue.

Peter's eyes narrow resentfully back onto the road.

The car passes a TELEPHONE POLE. Just an average telephone pole. But we HOLD on it for a second longer than feels necessary. *Hyper-attentive viewers might notice that a small SIGIL has been carved into it.*

EXT. PARTY HOUSE – NIGHT

A large modern house. The windows feature glimpses of a big party, filled with circulating kids.

Peter and Charlie walk up the driveway. Charlie, suddenly very nervous, starts slowing down.

CHARLIE
Maybe I don't have to go in…

Peter stops.

PETER
Why? What's wrong?

CHARLIE
It's okay. I can just stay out here.

PETER
Charlie, *you're* the one who wanted to come.

CHARLIE
(not looking at him)
So *you* just go. I'll be out here.

PETER

Charlie: if you don't come in, I have to take you back home, and that'll take an *hour*.

INT. PARTY HOUSE – MOMENTS LATER

The house is bustling. In the KITCHEN, two girls pull a CAKE from the oven. Another girl (working on the frosting) CHOPS up loads of WALNUTS on a chopping board.

ECU of the nuts being brutalized.

In the **LIVING ROOM**, Peter stands awkwardly with Charlie. Charlie grips her drawing pad.

AARON (17), a preppy-looking kid, walks suspiciously over to Peter. This is Aaron's house.

AARON

Hey.

PETER

Hey. Nice house.

AARON (CONT'D)

How did you hear about this?

PETER

Text.

Aaron nods, annoyed. He takes an aggressive sip of his drink. Peter is uncomfortable.

PETER (CONT'D)

(forcing conversation)

Your parents are out of town?

Peter suddenly spots BRIDGET across the room. She sits on the COUCH, obviously inebriated, nursing a beer. *Completely alone.*

AARON

You didn't bring beers or anything, did you?

Peter turns back to Aaron, very impatient now.

PETER

What? No.

(first thing that comes to mind)

I actually have to go to the bathroom.

Aaron nods *"yeah, whatever."* Peter, already backing away, turns to Charlie.

PETER (CONT'D)
Stay here one second, okay? I'm just going to the bathroom.

Peter starts walking. Charlie immediately follows. Peter feigns a trajectory toward the bathroom just behind Bridget. As he walks, he pretends to notice her. He affects a surprised face.

PETER (CONT'D)
Whoa, hey! What's up?

BRIDGET
Oh. Hey.

Peter steps toward her. A brief pause.

PETER
How's the party?

BRIDGET
(dry)

Why? You wanna know if you should come?

PETER
Uh — yeah. What do you think?

BRIDGET
(shrugs)
Whatever.

PETER
Okay, maybe I will.

BRIDGET
Okay, I'll see you here.

Another awkward pause.

PETER
Do you happen to smoke at all?

BRIDGET
Smoke what?

Peter pinches into his pocket. He reveals the top of a rolled-up BAG OF MARIJUANA.

BRIDGET (CONT'D)
(*"why not?"*)
I could get more high.

She stands up.

BRIDGET (CONT'D)
The other room has a bong.

PETER
Sick.

Bridget gestures for him to follow her. Peter starts to walk, but then notices Charlie following him.

PETER (CONT'D)
Hey. You wanna stay out here for a second?

CHARLIE
Nope.

PETER
Charlie: please. Only for two minutes and then we can hang out. You can draw.

Bridget is already at the DOOR to the other room. She looks expectantly at Peter, who turns again (desperately) to Charlie.

PETER (CONT'D)
Please, Charlie, I promise. I just need to do something really quick.

Peter then SEES something.

PETER (CONT'D)
Oh shit. Look:

He's pointing at the KITCHEN. The teen girls are now cutting into a fresh CHOCOLATE CAKE. They hand slices around.

PETER (CONT'D)
They're giving out chocolate cake.

CHARLIE
Not to everyone.

PETER (CONT'D)
Yes they are. It's a party.

CHARLIE (CONT'D)
I don't know anyone.

PETER

Nobody does. Just walk over, stand there, and they'll give you one.

Peter starts walking off, still facing Charlie:

PETER (CONT'D)

You should hurry, they're gonna run out, I'll be right back! Hurry!

Peter rushes over to Bridget as she OPENS the door to the other room. Charlie looks nervously to the kitchen.

INT. OTHER ROOM – CONTINUOUS

Two BOYS — one Hispanic and one blonde — are in the room, watching videos on a tablet. Bridget enters, addressing them:

BRIDGET

Hey guys, Peter has weed.

The boys turn to Peter. Peter immediately deflates.

HISPANIC BOY (O.S.)

Sativa or indica?

INT. KITCHEN – SAME TIME

Charlie steps into the doorway. Extremely shy. Her eyes are magnetized to the CHOCOLATE CAKE as the girls continue handing out slices.

One GIRL notices Charlie's fixed eyes. She warmly offers Charlie a slice. Charlie accepts without looking her in the eye.

CHARLIE

Thanks.

Charlie turns, digging into the cake. (Nuts are visibly a key ingredient.)

INT. OTHER ROOM – SAME TIME

Peter sits on the bed, beside Bridget. He packs marijuana into the bowl of a large bong.

BRIDGET

That was your sister, right?

PETER

Yeah. Charlie.

Peter's cell phone VIBRATES.

HISPANIC BOY

(to Peter)

Is your sister hot?

Peter checks the cell. It's ANNIE calling. Tense, he sets the phone down.

BRIDGET

I actually saw her drawing me last week.

PETER

Oh yeah?

BRIDGET

Yeah, she made me look retarded.

Peter's phone VIBRATES again. A yellow *"Message Waiting"* light blinks. Annie has left a VOICEMAIL.

INT. LIVING ROOM – SAME TIME

Charlie walks around, holding an empty plate, her lips covered in chocolate. She stops for a moment to SWALLOW. She pauses, then swallows again. She looks slightly concerned.

Charlie goes to a stack of RED CUPS and pulls one.

She goes to the kitchen faucet and draws herself a cup of water.

INT. ANNIE'S WORKSHOP – NIGHT

Annie is working on the miniature of the Graham house. She plants a freshly-painted FIGURINE of a ghostly old woman in a bath-robe (clearly Annie's MOTHER) in the upstairs hall. The figurine looms outside the open door of the master bedroom replica, where figurines of Annie and Steve are asleep in bed.

INT. PARTY HOUSE – LIVING ROOM – NIGHT

The party is still in full swing.

Charlie has found her way onto the COUCH and is now assembling a small manikin from disparate parts (from her pocket). Her cheeks look pink and slightly INFLAMED. *An allergic reaction to the cake?*

It looks like she's on the verge of throwing up, but she keeps her concentration on the manikin.

A concerned BOY (16) approaches Charlie. Not recognizing that she's a girl:

CONCERNED BOY (O.S.)
Hey dude, you okay? You want some water?

Charlie doesn't even look up.

CHARLIE
I'm okay.

CONCERNED BOY
You sure?

No answer. The boy hesitantly walks off.

Charlie does NOT look good.

INT. OTHER ROOM - MOMENTS LATER

Peter is drawing an impressive bong hit. The door is OPENED by Charlie.

CHARLIE
Peter?

This is just as Peter finishes inhaling. He COUGHS up smoke.

PETER
(like a chimney)
Charlie!

Peter immediately hides the bong behind his legs and looks to Charlie, affecting casualness.

PETER (CONT'D)
(still spouting smoke)
What's up?

Charlie looks scared.

PETER (CONT'D)
Are you okay?

CHARLIE
It's hard to breathe.

Charlie's voice is cracked and strange.

PETER
What do you mean?

CHARLIE
(tearing up)
My throat is getting bigger.

HARD CUT TO:

EXT. CAR – NIGHT

A distraught Peter pulls Charlie to the car. Charlie's eyes bulge and her face is pitch-red. She seems UNABLE TO BREATHE.

Peter desperately opens the back door, guides Charlie in, slams the door, and runs to the driver's side of the car.

INT. CAR (MOVING) – NIGHT

Peter speeds down the empty HIGHWAY. In the back seat, Charlie GASPS and gurgles for breath. She KICKS at the door and GRASPS at her throat. Tears of pain stream down her face.

Peter ACCELERATES. Speeding from 60 MPH to 65.

PETER
You're okay, Charlie! We're going to the hospital!

Charlie frantically rolls down her window. Desperate for air.

Peter continues accelerating. 70 MPH.

Charlie forces her head through the BACK PASSENGER WINDOW. She GASPS for breath, but her throat is swollen shut. She can't even scream.

Peter continues accelerating. 75 MPH.

Charlie sticks her squealing head even farther out the window.

Peter continues accelerating. 80… 85… But THEN –

A grisly DEER CARCASS, smeared across the road, appears in the car's headlights.

Peter SWERVES out of the way.

CHARLIE'S HEAD, flailing out of the window, COLLIDES FACE-FIRST WITH A TELEPHONE POLE. The impact is so great that Charlie's head is RIPPED OFF its shoulders.

The decapitated head SAILS silently in the car's wake.

Peter STOMPS on the brakes. The car SQUEALS to an ear-splitting halt.

The frozen car chugs quietly. Suspended in time.

Peter sits motionless. Paralyzed. His eyes are fixed on the road in front of him.

In the SIDE-VIEW MIRROR, the dead deer (thirty feet back) is faintly visible in the car's brake lights. Bathed in red.

Peter doesn't dare look back. His foot is jammed into the brake.

In the back seat, Charlie sits headless. A torso.

Peter's EYES begin to stray toward the REARVIEW MIRROR, but they STOP before they get there. Peter can't look.

Peter reaches for the rearview mirror and subtly turns it AWAY.

The *"Voicemail Waiting"* light (from Peter's cell) blinks through the fabric of his jeans pocket.

A long moment of silence, and then...

Peter's foot slowly eases OFF the brake pedal.

The car begins to slowly idle forward.

Peter, eyes locked on the road ahead, allows the car to slowly pick up speed. His demeanor suggests that he's in great denial. As if he's saying to himself *"it's okay, nothing happened."*

The car drives onward. The headless torso rattles gently in the back seat.

EXT. GRAHAM HOUSE – NIGHT

The car idles quietly into the driveway. It PARKS beside the other family car, but the engine continues humming.

The driver door opens, setting off the dull DING-DING-DING of the *"door open / engine on"* alarm. After a long pause, the engine is turned off. Peter steps out, as if in a dream state.

He walks stiffly away from the car and into the house.

INT. HALLWAY – CONTINUOUS

Peter stalks woodenly through the hall. He passes Annie and Steve's bedroom, behind whose closed door we hear:

ANNIE (O.S.)
Okay, good, they're home.

Peter enters his room, leaving the door open. He climbs into bed, fully clothed.

INT. BEDROOM – THE NEXT MORNING

The next morning.

CLOSE-UP on Peter's face, turned halfway into his pillow. His eyes are wide open.

Downstairs, we hear Annie pulling on her coat.

ANNIE (O.S.)
I'm running out for some balsa wood. You want anything?

STEVE (O.S.)
I'm good, baby. Drive safe.

ANNIE (O.S.)
Okay! Back in twenty!

The front door is heard opening and shutting. We then hear: Annie walking to the car… The car door opening… Annie beginning to climb in. And then… *Silence*. Followed by…

A horrible SCREAM, shrill and almost inhuman-sounding, issues from outside. Peter's eyes WIDEN. Annie is heard staggering backward and falling down, muttering (almost inaudibly) *"No, no, no, no…"* Downstairs (in the house), Steve is heard reacting and running to the front door. Before he makes it outside, Annie lets out another blood-curdling SHRIEK, which prompts a HARD CUT TO:

EXT. HIGHWAY – MORNING

CHARLIE'S HEAD rests by the side of the road. The nose is

completely smashed in. One eye is pitch-red and the other is milky and opaque. The head is completely covered in ANTS.

The halted shriek (from the last shot) ECHOES OFF into the wretched silence of *this* shot.

The sound of THUNDER bridges our cut to:

INT. GRAHAM HALLWAY - NIGHT

A STORM rages outside.

Annie and Steve's bedroom door is cracked open. We barely see ANNIE lying in bed, WEEPING and MOANING. Steve, sitting on the bed, consoles her. He tries to feed her a pill.

ANNIE

NO! I can't! I can't! I just wanna die!... I can't.

Steve rubs her head as she sinks into a more placid despair.

ANNIE (CONT'D)

... It hurts too much. I just need to die.

51 And then more feelings come SURGING up. She MOANS an anguished moan.

We reveal PETER, standing paralyzed in the hall, LISTENING. Annie's cries shred at his nerves.

ANNIE (O.S.) (CONT'D)

CHARLIE!!!

EXT. CEMETERY - DAY

An overcast day. A sad gathering of mourners. Annie, Peter, and Steve stand lost among them.

We are at a distance. The COFFIN (in profile) is being lowered into the ground. We are booming down to FOLLOW the sinking casket (keeping it centered), and as the coffin descends into the earth, *so do we.* We slowly creep down, losing sight of the cemetery and the mourners.

We continue tracking down along the DIRT and the EARTH-WORMS and the WEEDS, sinking deeper and deeper into the dark, wet soil. Soon we are swallowed up again in BLACK.

INT. HOUSE – LIVING ROOM – LATE AFTERNOON

THE WAKE. Everything seems slightly opaque, as if seen through glass. Glossed over by grief.

People stand uneasily and talk in hushed tones.

STEVE stands in a daze, politely (but absently) accepting condolences.

INT. ANNIE & STEVE'S BEDROOM – SAME TIME

Annie lies in bed, facing the wall. Her back is to us.

INT. LIBRARY – SAME TIME

Peter stands (hiding?) in the family library, anxiously massaging his CELL PHONE with his thumb. He looks completely battered by trauma and self-loathing.

He observes the wake in the adjacent living room through the distortion of the library's textured glass door. He watches Steve shake someone's hand.

52 A MAN (40s) steps into the library, not expecting to find Peter.

MAN
(surprised)
Peter. I'm so sorry.

Peter smiles politely. His eyes look almost deranged.

MAN (CONT'D)
Can I get you anything at all?

PETER
I'm just gonna use the bathroom.

MAN
Okay.

As Peter walks stiffly past, smiling his forced smile, the man awkwardly adds:

MAN (CONT'D)
I'm so sorry for your loss.

PETER
(exiting)
Thank you.

INT. BATHROOM – CONTINUOUS

Peter hastily enters the bathroom and LOCKS the door.

He stands frozen for a moment, battling panic. The sounds of the wake persist in the other room.

Peter turns on the SINK to create white noise.

INT. LIVING ROOM – EVENING

The remaining mourners are slowly filtering out. Steve politely ushers them, thanking them for coming.

Soon, everyone's gone. Steve just stands there, in the middle of the room. Lost.

INT. HALLWAY – MOMENTS LATER

Steve goes to the bathroom door. Tries to open it. It's LOCKED. The running sink is faintly heard.

Steve pauses, then knocks gently.

53 STEVE

Peter?

No answer.

INT. BATHROOM – SAME TIME

Peter sits on the edge of the tub. The sink is still running. He holds his cell to his ear, listening to a VOICEMAIL.

ROBOTIC FEMALE VOICE (V.O.)

You have one saved message. First saved message:

ANNIE (V.O.)

Hi, sweetheart, it's Mom. Just calling to make sure that you and Charlie are okay and having a good time at the BBQ. All right. Have lots of fun and be safe. Love you both!

Click.

ROBOTIC FEMALE VOICE (V.O.)

To listen to this message again, press four.

INT. ANNIE & STEVE'S BEDROOM – MOMENTS LATER

Steve approaches his bedroom, but STOPS at the open door.

Annie is no longer in bed. The sheets have been dragged halfway off the mattress (presumably by Annie's feet when she left).

INT. CHARLIE'S BEDROOM – MOMENTS LATER

Charlie's lonely bedroom. Everything is as it was.

The door OPENS. It's Steve. He stands at the door, taking the room in. After a moment, he steps inside.

MOMENTS LATER

Steve sits on Charlie's bed. He has pulled up Charlie's DRAWING PAD.

Steve opens the pad. He flips slowly through the pages. He takes care to really *look* at the drawings. As if appreciating them for the first time.

Steve passes several drawings of severed animal heads (including those of the rabbit, the rat, and the squirrel, which we saw in Charlie's shoebox). Steve then comes to Charlie's half-finished drawing of the pigeon head (which now dons a CROWN). Steve studies it, and then turns the page to discover... a BLANK PAGE. <u>There are no more drawings.</u>

The floodgates open. Steve WEEPS.

INT. CHARLIE'S BEDROOM – NIGHT

Charlie's bedroom is EMPTY again.

The door is open, and the hallway's lights are off.

Framed by the doorway, Peter walks past, determinedly <u>not</u> looking into the room.

INT. PETER'S BEDROOM – NIGHT

Peter enters. Without changing out of his clothes, he climbs into bed. The ALARM CLOCK reads *10:10 PM.*

He turns to his side and gazes out the WINDOW. The imposing TREEHOUSE looms just outside. He stares at it.

LATER

Peter rolls huffily from his stomach to his back, unable to sleep. He turns to the ALARM CLOCK. It now reads *1:32 AM.*

A beat, and then Peter climbs out of bed, gathers his blanket and pillow, and leaves the room.

EXT. GRAHAM HOUSE – MOMENTS LATER

Peter, wearing his parka and an Elmer Fudd hat, emerges from the back door of the house. He carries his blanket and pillow toward the TREEHOUSE.

He notes Charlie's SHOEBOX near the base of the tree (having been dropped from the treehouse?). Flies are audible inside.

Peter grips the tree's climbing handles and scales the tree.

INT. TREEHOUSE – CONTINUOUS

Peter climbs in. He lays out his blanket and lies down, positioning his pillow under his head. Now situated, he begins to close his eyes, but before they can shut, he SENSES something behind him.
55 He slowly looks back to SEE:

ANNIE IS SLEEPING IN THE CORNER, bundled up in blankets.

Startled, Peter STAGGERS out of his blanket, GRABS his things, and rushes frantically out of the treehouse. In his haste, his foot SLIPS OFF one of the climbing handles, he loses his grip, and he FALLS to land on his ass – HARD.

In pain, Peter rises and limps back toward the house.

WE SLOWLY DISSOLVE FROM THIS TO…

INT. CLASSROOM – DAY

Peter sits in the back of class as a teacher drones on at the blackboard. The teacher's voice is distant and vague, as if heard from UNDERWATER.

Peter's EYES are busy with nagging, obsessive thoughts. They narrow upward to his right.

We flash briefly to an **INSERT** of the family car's REARVIEW MIRROR (from Peter's POV) on the night of the accident. The mirror is in focus, but whatever's in the BACK SEAT (Charlie's headless body) is blurry and just out of the mirror's view.

We return to the CLASS. Peter snaps out of his reverie to see BRIDGET looking at him. Their eyes briefly MEET before she quickly turns back to the teacher.

Peter's eyes HARDEN.

EXT. GRAHAM HOUSE – DAY

Annie draws the MAIL out of the mailbox. Among the letters are two BROCHURES. One reads: *"Calling All Skeptics!"* Below that: *"A PUBLIC SEANCE to be conducted by famed spiritual medium, Suzanne Marlowe!"* The other brochure is for the *Grieving a Loved One* therapy group that Annie attended earlier.

Annie goes PALE at the sight of this. She looks around, suddenly paranoid that she's being watched.

INT. WORKSHOP – DAY

Annie is at work, trying to make progress on the HOSPICE MINIATURE. Her eyes are numb. She looks exhausted. She turns in her swivel-chair to face the miniature of the GRAHAM HOUSE. She stares at it.

Off-screen, the front door is heard UNLOCKING. Annie looks in the direction of the noise.

INT. FOYER – SAME TIME

The front door opens and Steve enters.

STEVE

Annie?!

Max runs up to greet Steve, his tail wagging excitedly.

INT. WORKSHOP – SAME TIME

Annie goes to the door. Steve is heard scaling the stairs. Before he can reach the top, Annie silently eases the door shut.

INT. HALLWAY – CONTINUOUS

The workshop door quietly CLOSES *just* before Steve appears at the top of the stairs. He approaches the workshop.

He knocks on the door.

No answer.

He eases the door open. Annie "works" with her back to the door. She's now wearing HEADPHONES, "listening" to classical music.

Steve smiles sadly and closes the door, leaving Annie to her work.

INT. KITCHEN – MOMENTS LATER

Steve enters the kitchen. Mail waits on the kitchen island. He finds the BROCHURE for the public seance, and DUMPS it in the trash.

In the b.g., Annie CROSSES the doorway. Steve doesn't see.

EXT. GRAHAM HOUSE – LATE AFTERNOON

Annie sits in the blue family car, parked in the driveway. *(The green car — the "accident" car — is now permanently gone.)* Annie is trying to work up the nerve to start the engine. Then, in the SIDE-VIEW MIRROR, she sees:

Peter rides his BICYCLE up the driveway. He arrives at the front porch, but stays on the bike. He doesn't see Annie.

Annie has TENSED UP. She sits motionless for fear of being seen, eyes LOCKED on Peter. He stands for a long time at the front door, preparing to face his family.

Annie watches as Peter continues to gather himself. He finally takes a decisive breath, gets off the bike, and quietly enters the house.

Annie remains tense. She turns on the car's IGNITION.

EXT. CATHOLIC HIGH SCHOOL GYMNASIUM – EVENING

Annie idles into the parking lot of the HIGH SCHOOL GYMNASIUM (from earlier). Outside, the same SUPPORT GROUP is gathering.

Annie pulls into a spot. Turns off the ignition. She stares at the gymnasium door. Watches tensely as people solemnly enter. She doesn't move.

After a long internal debate, Annie finally STARTS the car, backs up, and begins to drive off. As she approaches the exit, an OLDER WOMAN (late 60s) runs suddenly — and merrily — into the HEADLIGHTS, flagging Annie down. Annie BRAKES.

The woman circles over to Annie's window. Annie hesitantly rolls it down. The woman has very long, straight hair.

OLDER WOMAN
Hi! Hello. Sorry to chase you down.
(awkwardly)
Were you not coming in?

ANNIE
(cornered)
I, no, I just — forgot something.

OLDER WOMAN
Okay, sorry, I just — I recognized you from a few months ago. You were here because your mother?

ANNIE
Oh…

OLDER WOMAN
I feel crazy now. Sorry! I'm Joan.

ANNIE
(feeling trapped)
Hi.

JOAN
Are you doing any better?

ANNIE
What?

JOAN
With your mother…?

ANNIE
(still confused)
What?
(and then)
No. That's not… My daughter was killed.

JOAN
Oh. My God. I'm so, so sorry.

Brief, heavy silence. Joan stammeringly offers:

JOAN (CONT'D)
Would you like to come in with me? Or we can
(MORE)

even just get a coffee. There's a place down
the street.

ANNIE
I'm sorry. Really. Thank you.
(gesturing to leave)
I really did forget something.

Joan bluntly offers:

JOAN
My son died.

ANNIE
Oh...! I'm so sorry.

Joan smiles tightly, heartbroken.

JOAN
How old was yours?

Annie looks like she's being held hostage.

ANNIE
59 (pained to say it)
Thirteen.

JOAN
Oh God, that's awful!
(matter-of-fact)
My son and my grandson drowned. Four months
ago. The little one was seven.

ANNIE
(horrified)
Oh my God.

JOAN
I've been coming here for a month now and it *has*
helped. I just wanted to say. It has. It doesn't make
it easier — *obviously*. But sometimes it just, makes
it less lonely.

ANNIE
(awkwardly)
Okay...

JOAN

And I'm gonna embarrass myself now, but if you ever need someone to talk to...

Joan writes her PHONE NUMBER onto a piece of paper.

JOAN (CONT'D)

'Cause we all do.

She hands Annie the phone number.

JOAN (CONT'D)

Just if you need it.

ANNIE

Okay. Thank you. Really.

Annie is moved, despite her discomfort. Joan walks off, giving Annie a warm little wave.

INT. FOYER – NIGHT

Annie lumbers in. She pulls off her shoes.

60 INT. LIVING ROOM – MOMENTS LATER

Steve is asleep in an armchair, bathed in the dim glow of the muted TV. Annie appears in the doorway.

ANNIE

Hey.

STEVE

(waking up)

Oh! Hey.

ANNIE

I'm going to bed.

STEVE (CONT'D)

Where were you?

ANNIE (CONT'D)

At the movies. I'm going to bed.

STEVE

I'll come with you.

ANNIE

(put off)

... Okay.

Annie leaves the doorway.

STEVE

And can you please let me *know* when you're going to the movies? I was *worried.*

INT. ANNIE & STEVE'S BEDROOM – NIGHT

Annie and Steve are in bed. Annie's back is to Steve. Neither is asleep.

Steve gently SNUGGLES UP to Annie, but she is like stone. He self-consciously touches her hip. She recoils.

Steve backs off. There is a long moment of tension, and then Annie RISES from bed.

ANNIE

I'm gonna be right back.

She gathers a blanket, which is bundled on the room's armchair.

STEVE

You're *not* coming right back. You're taking the blanket.

ANNIE

I can't sleep.

STEVE

Annie: It's freezing outside.

ANNIE

The heater's up there.

Steve wants to fight this, but Annie is clearly anxious to avoid a conversation.

STEVE

... Okay.

ANNIE

Is that okay?

STEVE

(*"what am I supposed to say?"*)

Yeah. Fine. Come back if you get cold.

ANNIE

I just need to sleep.

Annie leaves.

INT. TREEHOUSE – NIGHT

We push in on an ominous WIDE of Annie lying asleep in Charlie's treehouse. Two LARGE HEATERS have been set up on either side of her. They burn a BRIGHT ORANGE.

INT. PETER'S BEDROOM – SAME TIME

Peter lies in bed, awake. Outside his window, Charlie's treehouse emits an orange glow.

A CLICKING SOUND (like Charlie's tongue-clicking) is suddenly heard in the room. Peter FREEZES, now listening for it. After a moment, there's another CLICK.

Peter BOLTS up in bed. His eyes frenziedly scan the room. He fixes on a DARK CORNER. A HOODIE SWEATSHIRT hangs on the wall, and for a brief moment, it looks *almost* like a standing person.

Peter continues listening intently for another click…

Silence. It has stopped.

INT. WORKSHOP – THE NEXT DAY

Outside, a beautiful day.

Inside, Annie is hard at work. Her eyes are intense — furious even — as she carefully works on the replica of Charlie's bedroom. She scratches a tiny replica of the word-carving she saw earlier (*"Satony"*) into the wall behind the bed. As she does this, her attention is drawn to a looming POST-IT NOTE, which reads:

Call gallery about extending?

Annie disregards this. She goes for a new bottle of paint, but as she reaches, an open paint bottle is KNOCKED over.

ANNIE

Shit.

It tipped over <u>near</u> Annie's extending hand, but it didn't *look* like Annie actually touched it.

Annie grabs paper towels and quickly mops up the mess. She pulls a few drenched items out of the widening paint puddle. Among them: JOAN'S PHONE NUMBER. She looks at it.

INT. HIGH SCHOOL HALLWAY – DAY

Peter walks absent-mindedly down the hall. THREE STONER BOYS (including Brendan) are walking toward him, huddled and giggling. They notice Peter.

BRENDAN

Yo, Pete.

PETER

Hey.

BRENDAN

(whispering)

You wanna join us for a walk?

On *"walk,"* he mimes pinching a joint with his thumb and forefinger.

EXT. HIGH SCHOOL SOCCER FIELD – DAY

Peter sits under the BLEACHERS with the three stoners. They pass around a PIPE packed with weed. Brendan takes a hit.

BRENDAN

(looking at his phone)

Am I the only one who's Facebook friends with Becky?

Brendan passes the pipe to Peter.

STONER #2

You're *friends* with Becky?

Peter holds the pipe. Stares at it.

BRENDAN

Facebook friends, bitch!

(back to his point)

Bro, her statuses…

STONER #3

Oh my God, dude, I know.

BRENDAN

Every ten seconds!

Peter LIGHTS the bowl and takes a reluctant hit.

BRENDAN (CONT'D)

5:45. "Think I'll go to the bathroom now." 5:46. "Just got back from the bathroom!"

Peter COUGHS OUT a lungful of pot smoke. He immediately looks regretful.

STONER #2
What about Brian with *his* girlfriend?

BRENDAN (CONT'D)
Ha! His "princess"?!

Stoner #2 nods his head, choking on laughter.

Peter's eyes are wide with a burgeoning panic. He does *not* look well.

STONER #2 (O.S.) (CONT'D)
"Going to pick up my princess from the airport!" "Eating couscous with my princess!"

Peter looks like he's starting to have an ATTACK. The Stoners are oblivious.

STONER #3
Who's his girlfriend?

STONER #2
Some fuckin' fat, stupid college chick.

STONER #3
What the fuck?! *I* want some stupid college princess chick.

Stoner #2 notices that Peter is freaking out.

STONER #2
Dude. Are you okay?

PETER
I feel like I can't breathe.

STONER #2
What?

PETER
I feel like I'm having a reaction.

BRENDAN
No, man, don't freak out. You just smoked too much.

PETER (CONT'D)
No, I think I need a doctor. <u>My tongue is getting bigger.</u>

Peter is crying now.

STONER #2
Should we take you to the nurse??

PETER
(scared)
I dunno.

BRENDAN
Look, dude: you're breathing. See? You're just really high.

Peter is trying to calm down.

BRENDAN (CONT'D)
See? You're okay. You just got too high.
(rubbing his back)
You're okay, dude. You're breathing.

Stoner #2 and Stoner #3 exchange *"holy shit"* looks.

EXT. STREET – DAY

Annie walks down an urban street, looking for an address. She pinches the paper with Joan's number. On its other side is an ADDRESS in
65 Annie's handwriting.

Annie finds the address. A large red-brick APARTMENT BUILDING.

INT. APARTMENT BUILDING – THIRD FLOOR HALLWAY – DAY

The elevator opens, depositing Annie onto the THIRD FLOOR. Annie proceeds down the well-lit hall, arriving at APARTMENT 316. She knocks.

While waiting, Annie looks down. She's standing on a HAND-MADE WELCOME MAT. The word *"JOANIE"* has been embroidered into it.

After a moment, the door is opened by JOAN.

JOAN
Annie! You came!

ANNIE
It's a little earlier than we said.

JOAN (CONT'D)
Ah, you're perfect. Come in.

INT. JOAN'S APARTMENT – CONTINUOUS

Annie follows Joan in. Joan closes the door behind them. The apartment is cheerfully decorated in bright, homey colors.

Joan rushes off to the KITCHEN, where a TEA KETTLE is whistling. Annie stays by the door.

ANNIE

Your welcome mat...

JOAN

Oh — it's cute, right?

Joan pulls the kettle off the stove and pours two cups.

ANNIE

My mother used to embroider ones just like that.

JOAN

Oh really? How funny!

Joan sets the tea on the KITCHEN table.

JOAN (CONT'D)

Please. Sit.

MINUTES LATER

Joan and Annie sit at the table, nursing their tea. The conversation has become very heavy, and the spotlight is currently on a very fragile Annie. She speaks steadily, in fragments, as if to hold herself together. Her eyes are fixed on the table.

ANNIE

He left her in the back seat. Went straight to bed.

Joan nods sympathetically. Her eyes locked attentively on Annie.

ANNIE (CONT'D)

And then *I* wake up. Went to my workshop. Needed some supplies. I go down to the car. Step inside. First the smell of something wrong. Then the — body. Slumped. Covered in black blood, like *tar*...

(fighting tears)

And her head wasn't there, so there was no face. But they were her clothes. And her hands... her fingernails...

Joan is pale as she listens. Annie is trembling, locked on the memory.

Joan gently lays her hand over Annie's. Beat.

JOAN

When they dragged up my son and grandson, they needed me to identify the bodies. But they didn't warn me what bodies *look* like after they've been in the ocean. You can probably imagine — they swell up, get distended, turn gray. *I* didn't know that. My son's eyes were eaten out of his head by fish. And my grandson's face — like a balloon.

Annie is looking up at Joan now. They share in this. The grisly details are somehow (in their morbid way) comforting.

Breaking the spell, Annie pulls a PILL from her purse. She downs it with a gulp of TEA. She catches something on her tongue, and pulls a BLACK HERB from her mouth. She pays it no mind.

JOAN (CONT'D)

I can sometimes *swear* I feel them in the room... Do you ever have that?

67 ANNIE

... Small moments maybe.

This hangs for a moment.

JOAN

How's your relationship with your son?

ANNIE

... Peter?

Joan brightens: *"That's his name?"*

ANNIE (CONT'D)

Oh God...

Annie's face DARKENS and she chuckles. She brushes off the question, but then PAUSES. She decides to actually answer.

ANNIE (CONT'D)

I sleepwalk.

(pause)

I haven't in a long time, but two years ago I woke up — and I really *don't* remember this because I

(MORE)

was *asleep* — but I woke up standing next to Peter and Charlie's bed (when they shared a room), and they were *completely* covered in paint thinner… And so was I. From head to toe… And I was standing there, and I was holding a box of matches… and an *empty* can of paint thinner … and I woke myself up by *striking* a match. Which also woke up *Peter.* And he started screaming. And I immediately put out the match, *immediately*, but my husband came in… And I was just as shocked as *he* was, but *I* was the one with the matches.

Joan is listening with no judgment. Annie, frustrated by the memory, takes a deep breath.

ANNIE (CONT'D)

And it was impossible to convince them that it was *just* sleepwalking — which of *course* it was — but the timing was awful, Peter and I had already fallen into this stupid quarrelling phase — arguing forever about *nothing* — such *frivolous things* — but that's when the incident happened, *so…!*

(throws her hands up)

Over time, everyone *affected* casualness, "moving on." But they never forgot and Peter's *always* held it against me and there's nothing I can *say* and there's nothing I can *do* because it *happened.* While I was asleep.

JOAN

Did your daughter hold it against you?

ANNIE

Oh, she was off in the clouds somewhere. Probably didn't even notice.

INT. GRAHAM HOUSE - KITCHEN - MOMENTS LATER

Steve is chopping carrots at the kitchen island. Peter is heard ENTERING in the foyer.

STEVE

Hey, that was fast. Did you bike all the way here?

PETER

(voice cracked)

My friend dropped me.

STEVE

Oh — you should've invited him in.

But Peter's already going for the stairs. Steve tries to catch up with him.

STEVE (CONT'D)

Did you remember to sign up for that SAT prep course?

Peter has made it to the top of the stairs. Hiding his wrought face:

PETER

I will tomorrow.

STEVE (CONT'D)

You need to, Peter! That's coming up!

INT. PETER'S ROOM – DAY

Peter lies in bed, on his side. He looks ready to burst back into tears.

Steve knocks on the door. Pokes his head in.

STEVE

Peter?

Peter turns to him, stifling tears.

STEVE (CONT'D)

Are you okay?

PETER

(deflecting)

Are *you?*

Pause.

STEVE

Is there anything we can talk about?

PETER

Like what?

STEVE

Like anything. What's going on? What are you feeling?

PETER

What are *you* feeling?

STEVE

I'm worried about you.

Peter stares at Steve, eyes wide. Unable to communicate.

STEVE (CONT'D)

(careful)

It doesn't have to be with *me*, either. Maybe you'd like to talk with somebody else...

PETER

About *what?*

STEVE

About everything. You're going through a lot.

PETER

So are you!

STEVE

Well — we *all* are. I think we could *all* use someone to talk to.

PETER

(on "talk")

So why aren't *you*, then?

STEVE

I probably *will*. I probably *need* to.

A long, fraught pause.

STEVE (CONT'D)

You don't have to choose now. I'm just letting you know that it's *there*. You could even see one of the guys in my *building*. I know a *few* guys.

PETER

(warming up to it?)

...And *you* think I *need* to go?

STEVE

(briefest pause)

Well, that's for *you* to say. I can't tell you your experience.

Peter suddenly deflates. *Not the answer he needed*. He chills over.

PETER

Maybe later.

STEVE

... Okay. Let me know.

PETER

Okay.

Steve nods for a long time. Trying to think of anything else.

STEVE

All right. Dinner in a bit.

Steve smiles sensitively. *Too* sensitive. He leaves.

INT. WORKSHOP – NIGHT

Annie is at work. Behind her, the door opens and Steve enters.
He approaches to see...

Annie is working on a new piece: a MINIATURE of the HIGHWAY
of Charlie's accident, including the TELEPHONE POLE that took
her head. This also features a tiny figurine of Charlie's decapitated
71 head and a figurine of Peter in the family car.

STEVE

Jesus, Annie. Are you planning on letting him see that?

ANNIE

Who?

STEVE

(strong pause)

How do you think *Peter's* gonna feel about that?

ANNIE

What? It's not *about* him.

STEVE	ANNIE (CONT'D)
Oh, no?	It's a neutral view of the accident!

Steve just eyes her.

ANNIE (CONT'D)

Okay, so what *is* it, then?

STEVE
It's cruel, Annie. And unforgiving...

ANNIE (CONT'D)
Oh my *God!*

STEVE
And *use*less.

ANNIE
(incredulous)
What do you think I'm trying to *say* with this?! You think I'd ever want to hurt my own *son?!* Are you *crazy?!*

Steve almost responds, but bites his tongue.

ANNIE (CONT'D)
Oh *Jesus* you're sanctimonious. I get it: you're a good father, you're a good husband — get off the stage.

Steve boils.

STEVE
(through clenched teeth)
Are you coming to dinner?

ANNIE
I'm *making* dinner!

STEVE
(snapping)
I made dinner! I'm GETTING you for dinner!
(storms away)
Come down or stay here, I don't *give* a shit.

On "give," he SLAMS the door behind him.

INT. DINING ROOM - NIGHT

Annie, Steve, and Peter sit at the dinner table. A fourth chair divides Annie and Peter. Annie is fuming from her last interaction with Steve. Beside her glass: an unswallowed pill.

PETER
This is really good, Dad.

Annie balks to herself. Peter tenses.

STEVE

Thanks, buddy.

Annie mouths the word *"buddy"* to herself, incredulous. Peter catches this.

PETER

(with an edge)

You okay, Mom?

Annie turns to Peter.

ANNIE

What?

PETER

Is there something on your mind?

Annie can't believe this.

ANNIE

Is there something on *your* mind?

PETER

It just looks like you might want to say something.

STEVE

(stepping in)

Peter...

ANNIE

Like *what?* Why would I want to *say* something?
So I can watch you roll your eyes at me?

PETER	ANNIE (CONT'D)
I have *never* rolled my eyes at you.	Oh sweetie — you don't *have* to. You get the point across.

PETER (CONT'D)

(suddenly defiant)

Okay. So say what you wanna say, then.

STEVE

Peter —

ANNIE

(getting angry)

I don't <u>want</u> to say anything. I've <u>tried</u> saying things.

PETER

So try again. Release yourself.

ANNIE

Release *you*, you mean!

PETER (CONT'D)

So fine, so release me! What do you wanna say? Fuckin' say it!

Annie explodes out of her seat.

ANNIE

Don't you swear at me — you little *shit!* You don't EVER raise your voice at me! I am your *Mother*, you understand? I've given *everything* to you! All I ever *DO* is worry and slave and defend you, and all I get back is that fucking face on your face! So full of disdain and resentment and always so *annoyed*. Well, now your sister's dead! And I *know* you miss her and I *know* it was an "accident" and I *know* you're in pain — and I wish I could take it all away! I wish I could shield you from the knowledge that you did what you did — but your sister is *dead*. She's gone forever. And what a *waste*. If it could've maybe brought us together — *something!* — if you could have just said "I'm sorry" or faced *up* to what happened: maybe *then* we could *do* something with this! *But you can't take responsibility for anything!* So now I can't accept. And I can't forgive. Because nobody admits what they've done!

She sits down. A heavy silence.

Peter is looking away, fighting tears. But then, after a long silence...

PETER

And what about *you*, Mom?

(long pause, then)

I didn't want to take her... and *she* didn't want to go... So why was she there?

Annie looks at him. Incredulous. She is boiling with rage, **but...** this has also hit her somewhere *deep*. She's desperately avoided facing this question since the accident.

STEVE

Okay, we're stopping this.

He looks at Annie, who looks like she's about to lose it.

STEVE (CONT'D)
We're stopping this right now.

Annie glowers at him. Adversarial. She finally relents.

ANNIE
Fine.

She tensely RISES, but then hesitates, about to say something else. But then:

ANNIE (CONT'D)
Fine.

She leaves.

Steve turns to Peter: he's doing everything in his power to keep from exploding into tears. Steve looks powerless to help.

INT. ANNIE & STEVE'S BEDROOM – MINUTES LATER

Steve enters the bedroom, furious. Annie is sitting on the bed, a hardness in her eyes.

75 STEVE
What the hell are you doing?

ANNIE
What am *I* doing?!

STEVE
Try to stop and see what's happening, Annie. For *one* second. Try to see where this could go. It's *not* the right choice.

ANNIE
These are *your* choices, too! You *choose* to not see how he is. How *cold* he is with me. How dismissive.

STEVE
So we'll deal with that! We can go to family therapy, whatever — but *don't* make it about *Charlie!*

ANNIE (CONT'D)
Oh, family therapy! Right!

ANNIE (CONT'D)
So what, then? We just chalk it up to an act of God?

STEVE

(strongly)

Yes.

<table>
<tr><td>ANNIE
He just left her in the car!
Went straight to bed! Not a word!</td><td>STEVE (CONT'D)
You can't even imagine he was in shock?</td></tr>
</table>

ANNIE

He left *us* to be in shock, too!

STEVE

There was no way around that. You need to stop this. If he *had* warned us, we still would have run out there to find her in the same way.

ANNIE

(ignoring him)

And it wasn't a fucking BBQ either. He lied to us, through his *teeth.* He took her to some sleazy high school house party!

<table>
<tr><td>STEVE
You knew it wasn't a BBQ!</td><td>ANNIE (CONT'D)
He just left her head in the road and kept driving. He went to sleep!</td></tr>
</table>

STEVE

Goddamn it — he was in <u>shock</u>. He's *still* in shock.

ANNIE

(acidly)

He looks pretty gathered to me.

<table>
<tr><td>STEVE
Gathered?!</td><td>ANNIE (CONT'D)
You're holding yourself together awfully well, too!</td></tr>
</table>

STEVE

Excuse me? And what the hell does *that* mean?

(no answer)

Someone has to keep things from unraveling *completely*, Annie.

ANNIE

(exploding)

It HAS unraveled completely!

Silence. Steve is frozen.

ANNIE (CONT'D)
... Don't worry. I blame myself, too.

STEVE
That's worthless.

ANNIE
I'm the one who made her go to the party.

STEVE
Oh, stop it!

ANNIE (CONT'D)
No! Don't you *dare!* He's right! I made Peter take her! She *begged* me not to go!

STEVE
I was *happy* she was going! Be around other kids instead of that fuckin' treehouse for a change!

Annie is just shaking her head.

STEVE (CONT'D)
... We have no control over anything, Annie. The ceiling could collapse on us right now and who would we blame?

Brief pause.

ANNIE
You don't understand anything, do you?

INT. PETER'S BEDROOM – NIGHT

Peter boils in bed, staring out the window.

A gentle knock at the door. It cracks open and Steve sticks his head in.

STEVE
Goodnight, Petey.

Peter looks at Steve.

PETER
Do *you* blame me, too?

STEVE
Goddamn it —

Steve opens the door all the way.

STEVE (CONT'D)
— of course not. No one blames you.

Steve approaches Peter.

STEVE (CONT'D)
I don't for one *second* imagine that you're not going through the *exact* same thing we are.

PETER
Mom doesn't think so.

STEVE
Stop it with Mom. She's blaming everyone. It's part of grieving. She blames herself.

Peter has started to cry.

PETER
She wasn't driving the car.

STEVE
She *could* have. Anyone could have.

PETER
(through helpless tears)
I didn't even care about her...! That's how it happened...!

Steve is momentarily overwhelmed.

STEVE
(weakly)
You love your sister.

PETER
(boiling with self-hatred)
I should be dead. At least she could draw. She *made* things. I don't do *any*thing.

STEVE
Yes you do. Don't ever say that.

PETER
(burying his face in his pillow)
I'm *nothing*. I do *nothing*.

Steve, looking helpless, rests his hand on Peter's head. Peter WEEPS. Steve is also crying now.

PETER (CONT'D)
(into his pillow)
I'm sorry!

STEVE
Shhh! *I'm* sorry.

INT. ANNIE & STEVE'S BEDROOM – SAME TIME

Annie lies on the bed, her back to us. We hear Peter's weeping, muffled through the walls. We then hear:

ANNIE
(barely audible)
I'm sorry.

Annie's back begins to rise and fall in a fit of sobs.

FADE TO BLACK

INT. WORKSHOP – DAY – DAYS LATER

CLOSE-UP of Annie's face. Lethargic. She's lost a few pounds since we last saw her and is wearing an old T-shirt and pajama bottoms.

She stares at her unfinished miniatures. Her eyes then drift to a Post-it note above her desk. It reads *"KEEP WORKING!"*

INT. ART SUPPLY STORE – DAY

Annie emerges from an art supply store carrying two bags of miniature building material. As she approaches the PARKING LOT, she suddenly freezes, having just noticed...

JOAN is at her car, loading the trunk with recently purchased items. She hasn't yet noticed Annie. She wears an ECSTATIC SMILE as she giddily unloads a chalkboard (and accompanying chalk) from her cart.

Confused by Joan's demeanor (and her presence), Annie warily approaches her.

ANNIE
Joan?

Joan looks up to see Annie.

JOAN
Oh my — Annie?!

ANNIE

Hi…!

Joan rushes to give Annie a big, warm, very sustained HUG.

ANNIE (CONT'D)

Are you okay?

JOAN

(beaming)

Oh, Annie. Yes. I'm really good. I'm really really…

Annie forces a smile. She looks concerned for Joan's sanity.

JOAN (CONT'D)

Something happened, Annie. I feel completely — turned around.

ANNIE

What happened?

JOAN

(laughing)

I don't know if I should even say!

ANNIE

(laughing now, too)

What do you mean?

JOAN

You're gonna think I'm crazy!

ANNIE

Not at all…!

JOAN

I… oh God. I…

(confidentially)

… met a spiritual medium.

Now doubly concerned, Annie affects a patronizing *"oh wow"* expression.

JOAN (CONT'D)

(explaining)

They were performing an open seance — and I know: I know what you're thinking, but they asked me to attend, they were bringing in skeptics and

(MORE)

scientists so they wouldn't be accused of fraud, and I went, *fully* skeptical, but what I experienced there was truly...

Joan tries to think of a suitably ecstatic adjective.

ANNIE
An "open seance"?

JOAN
They brought back the spirit of a man from the nineteenth century! And *not* like as a smoke and mirrors thing! I know what you're thinking! The man next to me was a deadly cynical *neurologist*, and he looked totally *changed* by the end of this.

Annie makes another *"wow"* face.

JOAN (CONT'D)
I do know what you're thinking, Annie — of *course* — but I approached the medium afterwards and I asked her about my son and my grandson, and she came to my apartment and she ended up, uh, performing a, uh... well — she... *conjured* my grandson!

Annie, still forcing a smile, now looks frightened.

JOAN (CONT'D)
I know what you're smiling at. I wouldn't believe it myself. I *didn't!* But I *heard* his voice, I *felt* him in the room. It's *real.*

Annie's warped smile is plastered appeasingly to her face.

JOAN (CONT'D)
What are you doing right now?

ANNIE
I'm just — here, shopping.

JOAN
You wanna come over?

Annie doesn't know what to say.

JOAN (CONT'D)
I really think you should. Please. It would be everything if you came.

INT. JOAN'S APARTMENT – DAY

The front door opens and Joan enters, followed uneasily by Annie. Joan smiles widely.

JOAN

Hello!

This "hello" was seemingly directed at the room in general.

Joan hustles to the KITCHEN. She takes SWEETGRASS and smears it across the surface of the kitchen table. Also on the table is an UPTURNED DRINKING GLASS.

JOAN (CONT'D)

(to Annie)

This is part of it.

Annie is hovering outside the kitchen.

JOAN (CONT'D)

Come in. Come in.

Annie hesitantly enters. The WINDOW has been blacked out by a thick blanket.

JOAN (CONT'D)

Okay: a few things. *First:* you shouldn't do this without a medium unless you <u>are</u> a medium. That's what she told me.

ANNIE

Okay.

JOAN

But I told you: I'd been experiencing these... sensations a long time *before* the medium. I just didn't know how to explain them! So I tried this last night. This was *after* the medium was here.

ANNIE

What's "this"?

JOAN

Sit down.

Annie is skeptical.

JOAN (CONT'D)

Trust me.

Annie sits down.

JOAN (CONT'D)

I'm turning off the light.

JOAN TURNS OFF THE LIGHTS.

JOAN (CONT'D)

You okay?

ANNIE

... Yes.

Joan lights a BLACK CANDLE.

ANNIE (CONT'D)

(forcing levity)

Nice mood setter.

JOAN

Okay. Put your hand on the glass, but don't add pressure.

Annie lays her hand on the overturned glass. Joan does the same.

JOAN (CONT'D)

I won't add pressure, either.

ANNIE

(more to herself)

What am I doing?

After a moment of silence, Joan speaks to the room.

JOAN

Louie?

Beat.

JOAN (CONT'D)

Louie, are you here? It's Grandma.

A COLD DRAFT crosses the room. Annie gets a tingle. But the window is shut, as is the door.

JOAN (CONT'D)

Louie, if you're here with us, please just try to slide the glass.

(pause)

Louie, if you're here —

The glass SLIDES, barely. Annie jumps, retracting her hand.

JOAN (CONT'D)

(tears of happiness)

Hi, Louie!

ANNIE

(eyes wide)

How did you do that?

Annie looks under the table. There's nothing there.

JOAN

(continuing)

Louie, I'm gonna ask you some questions — okay, sweetie? If the answer's yes, just slide the glass to the right. If it's no, slide it *this* way —

(demonstrating)

— to the left. Do you understand?

The glass SLIDES again, slightly to the right.

ANNIE

Oh my God.

JOAN

Louie, are you okay?

The glass slides right again.

JOAN (CONT'D)

Are you in pain?

The glass slides to the left.

Annie is gripping her chair. She stares unblinkingly at the glass.

Suddenly ANNIE'S HAIR IS BRUSHED TO THE SIDE, as if by an invisible hand. She JUMPS. Joan calmly takes Annie's hand.

JOAN (CONT'D)

It's okay.

ANNIE

(frightened)

What is?

Joan pulls up a small CHALKBOARD from below the table. It's unmarked. A tiny piece of chalk rests on the surface.

JOAN

Louie, I brought your chalkboard. Remember your chalkboard?

The glass budges slightly to the right.

JOAN (CONT'D)

Can you write something?

A long moment of inactivity, and THEN...

The piece of chalk MOVES (as if by invisible fingers) to scrawl the words *"I LUV YU GRANMA"* in a young child's handwriting!

JOAN (CONT'D)

Oh, Louie, I love *you*, sweetheart!

Joan is crying tears of joy.

ANNIE

I'm sorry, can we stop?

JOAN

What?

ANNIE

I'm sorry. Please.

JOAN

(to the room)

Louie, we're gonna stop for a second, but I'm coming right back!

Joan jumps up and turns on the lights. Annie looks rattled.

JOAN (CONT'D)

Are you okay?

ANNIE

(shaken)

I'm sorry, I'm really...

JOAN

I understand. That's how *I* reacted at first.

ANNIE

I think I need to go.

JOAN

That's okay.

ANNIE (CONT'D)

Thank you. I'm sorry.

Annie RISES. Joan blows out the candle, grabs it, and shuffles to the kitchen to fetch a sheet of paper. It features a Sanskrit prayer (transcribed in carefully handwritten English).

Joan returns to Annie with the paper and the black candle.

JOAN

Here:

(handing them to her)

If you wanna try this yourself, light the candle and choose one item that belonged to your daughter — that'll be your link to her. Mine was the chalkboard. That's my link. And then, when you're ready —

(seriously, re: the paper)

— read this out loud — *every* syllable — *very* carefully.

ANNIE

(overwhelmed)

Why? What is it?

JOAN

I don't know what language it is. The medium had *me* read it, too. It's to make it start. But your whole family — everyone — needs to be in the room. Your son. Everyone.

Annie uneasily accepts the articles and then turns to leave. As she walks toward the door:

JOAN (CONT'D)

You didn't kill her, Annie.

Annie turns sharply to Joan.

ANNIE

What?

JOAN
She isn't gone.

ANNIE
I *didn't* kill her!

Joan smiles warmly. *"I know."*

ANNIE (CONT'D)
Okay. Thank you.

Annie leaves, trembling.

INT. CAR (MOVING) - EVENING

A discombobulated Annie drives back home. Her eyes are buzzing and her movements are jerky and ill-possessed.

She slows to a stop at a red light.

As she sits waiting for the light to change, Annie hears a CLICKING SOUND in the back seat. She goes white, and turns to look at the EMPTY back seat. The clicking has ceased.

87 Annie's eyes are crazed.

EXT. GRAHAM HOUSE - NIGHT

A wide shot of the house. Bathed in the pale moonlight, it almost looks like one of Annie's miniatures. All the lights are off, save for ONE window.

INT. ANNIE & STEVE'S BEDROOM - SAME TIME

Steve is fast asleep. Annie's side of the bed is EMPTY.

The door to the MASTER BATHROOM is closed, but a band of light is visible beneath the door. Behind the door, Annie is heard WHISPERING intensely — presumably on the phone.

ANNIE (O.S.)
Can it be anything?... Like her clothes?

INT. PETER'S BEDROOM - NIGHT

CLOSE-UP on Peter's profile. He's asleep.

Off-screen, the door is heard CREAKING OPEN. After a moment, Annie leans into frame, hovering over Peter.

ANNIE
(whispering)
Peter.

Peter doesn't stir.

ANNIE (CONT'D)
Sweetheart. Peter. Wake up.

Peter INHALES sharply. He wakes with a start.

PETER
What?

ANNIE
It's okay, honey, it's me.

Peter is very disoriented. Annie looks strangely hopeful.

ANNIE (CONT'D)
I'm so, so sorry for everything. Please, *please* forgive me. I can't *stand* the things I said.

PETER
It's okay.

Annie bends over to envelop him in a hug.

ANNIE
Can you get up, sweetheart? We're gonna try something.

PETER
I was just having a nightmare.

ANNIE
That's okay, baby. We can do something.

PETER
Do what?

ANNIE
I've figured it out.

INT. ANNIE & STEVE'S BEDROOM – MOMENTS LATER

Annie stands over Steve, who's asleep in bed.

ANNIE

Steve. Baby.

She nudges him gently.

ANNIE (CONT'D)

Steve. Wake up.

Steve jolts awake.

STEVE

What's going on?

ANNIE

Come downstairs with us. We're gonna do something together.

Steve looks to the door. Peter is standing nervously in the unlit hallway.

INT. HALLWAY – MOMENTS LATER

Annie walks down the hall. Steve and Peter follow warily behind.

89 PETER

(whispering)

Dad?

STEVE

(whispering)

It's okay.

Annie leads them to the unlit DINING ROOM...

INT. DINING ROOM – CONTINUOUS

The oval dining table has been set with an upturned DRINKING GLASS. Beside it is CHARLIE'S DRAWING PAD and one of Charlie's hoodies. The BLACK CANDLE that Joan gave Annie is dimly illuminating the table. The WINDOW is open, and it is COLD. Peter hugs himself; Steve rubs his arms.

STEVE

It's freezing.

Steve goes for the window.

ANNIE

No: *hey:* don't change anything. I don't want to mess it up.

Steve stops midway to the window. Annie sits down. There are chairs on either side of her.

ANNIE (CONT'D)

Everyone sit.

They don't.

ANNIE (CONT'D)

My friend Joan taught me how to do this.

STEVE

What friend Joan? And what's *"this"*?

ANNIE

Please sit. We need our palms on the table and our fingers to touch.

STEVE	ANNIE (CONT'D)
What are we doing, Annie?	Please. You'll see.

Steve just looks at her.

ANNIE (CONT'D)

Please just trust me.

Steve doesn't budge.

ANNIE (CONT'D)

Fine!

Annie stands up, DRAGS the table towards Peter. She then marches to Steve, grabbing his hand, and pulls him to the table.

ANNIE (CONT'D)

We can do it *here*, then.

She SQUEEZES their hands.

ANNIE (CONT'D)

I need you both to concentrate.

PETER

On what?

ANNIE

(pause)

Think about Charlie if you can.

STEVE

(stern)

Annie!

Steve pulls his hand away from Annie.

ANNIE

(urgent)

Honey, please. *Please.* I tried this twenty minutes ago and it *worked.* I wouldn't be bringing you down here if it didn't.

STEVE

What worked?

ANNIE

(pause)

I wanna just show you.

STEVE

91 Show us what?!

ANNIE

(frustrated)

Fuck! I'm a — medium!

Before Steve can protest:

ANNIE (CONT'D)

I was seeing apparitions earlier. I just shook them off, but I *shouldn't* have.

(gripping his hand)

Please: I know how it sounds. There's no way to talk about it, I need to just *show* you. Okay? *Please.* You'll see. I'm completely lucid.

Steve just stares at her. She looks pleadingly at him.

STEVE

(to Peter)

You can go to bed, Peter. I'll stay.

ANNIE (CONT'D)

What? *No.* What are you doing?

(to Peter)

Peter: please. This needs *all* of our

(MORE)

energies. We need
to do this as a *family.*
Together.

PETER

(to Steve)

It's okay, Dad. I'll stay.

ANNIE

(to Steve)

Please, Steve. I need you to be open. Both of you.
I promise.

She holds out her hand, pleading for Steve's. He reluctantly obliges. Again, she SQUEEZES both of their hands.

ANNIE (CONT'D)

Okay, good. So I already read *that* earlier...

Annie nods to the prayer sheet that Joan gave her.

ANNIE (CONT'D)

I don't think I need to read it again.

Steve squints as he looks it over.

STEVE

What *language* is that?

ANNIE (CONT'D)

(back to business)

Okay: try to concentrate.

Annie now addresses the room.

ANNIE (CONT'D)

Charlie?... Charlie, are you here?

Steve looks ready to put an immediate stop to this, but he sees Annie's total determination. He holds off.

ANNIE (CONT'D)

Charlie, it's Mommy. And Daddy. And Peter.

Behind Peter, a CREAKING sound is heard. Peter looks in that direction.

ANNIE (CONT'D)

Charlie, if you're in this room with us — I'm going
to have us all touch this glass.

Annie takes Steve's hand and Peter's hand and lays them on top of the glass. She places her hand atop theirs.

ANNIE (CONT'D)
(to Steve and Peter)
Don't add pressure.
(to the room)
Now if you're here, Charlie, I just want you to move the glass for us. Even if it's just a tiny little bit.

STEVE
(needing to interject)
Annie.

ANNIE (CONT'D)
(ignoring Steve)
Even if it's just the tiniest little movement, Charlie!

A long stretch of nothing. Annie's determination has not waned. Peter suddenly TENSES UP.

PETER
(to Steve)
What the hell?

STEVE

What's wrong?

Max BARKS in the other room.

PETER
You don't feel that?

STEVE
What??

PETER
In the air. Like a — flexing.

THE DRINKING GLASS SUDDENLY MOVES OF ITS OWN ACCORD! Peter and Steve retract their hands as the glass slides across the table.

STEVE
What the hell?

ANNIE
Wow! Yes! Thank you, Charlie! That was so good!

The color has drained from Peter's face.

ANNIE (CONT'D)
Now, Charlie, what I'd like for you to do is, I'd like for you to...

Annie opens the DRAWING PAD. She flips it to a blank page and lays a small piece of PENCIL LEAD on top.

ANNIE (CONT'D)
... show them what you were doing earlier.

Pause.

ANNIE (CONT'D)
(to the room)
Can you show them what you just did for me?

PETER
Mom.

Intensely focused, Annie points to the pad.

ANNIE
Look: she's gonna do it.

Peter looks to the pad, terrified. Steve SEES Peter's fear. Steve SHUTS the drawing pad.

STEVE
That's enough.

ANNIE
What? No!

Annie grabs the pad and flips to a PAGE near the back. It is a simple DRAWING — in Charlie's style — of a CAR. She holds it up for Steve.

ANNIE (CONT'D)
When I did this earlier, *this* materialized on the page! I saw this draw *itself!* I *saw* it!

PETER
Mom, what is this?

ANNIE
IT'S CHARLIE!

STEVE
ANNIE —

Cutting Steve off, Annie continues addressing the room.

ANNIE
Did you finish, Charlie?! Did you want to draw more?

She returns the drawing pad (now open to the car drawing) to the center of the table.

ANNIE (CONT'D)
You can keep going if you weren't finished!

Annie GRABS Steve's and Peter's hands and presses them against the table again. She pushes her hands on top of theirs.

ANNIE (CONT'D)
We need to keep our fingers touching. We need to give good energy.

Steve PULLS his hand away. Peter does too. Annie SEIZES Peter's wrist.

STEVE
This is SCARING him Annie!

ANNIE (CONT'D)
No it's NOT!

ANNIE (CONT'D)
(to Peter)
Don't be scared, Peter. This is your sister.
(to the room)
Charlie? Are you finished with the drawing?

Silence. Suddenly an intense GUST OF AIR sweeps the room (from the open window?) and a CUPBOARD DOOR SLAMS SHUT. Max is now BARKING like crazy in the other room.

PETER
(very scared)
Mom?!

ANNIE
(to the room)
Charlie? What's wrong?

The air seems to be sucked out of the room for a moment. The family is suspended in frightened anticipation. And then —

THE CANDLE'S FLAME BELCHES, as if fueled (for an instant) by propane. Everyone GASPS! The flame is immediately extinguished.

Silence now — save for Max, still barking in the other room. We are left for a moment in darkness, and then...

The candle's wick quietly REIGNITES on its own. The flame now burns normally. Peter and Steve stare open-mouthed at this.

Steve looks under the table. Nothing is there. He warily lifts the candle to see if there's anything attached to the bottom. There is not. Before Steve can react —

A FAINT GROANING SOUND is ushered. Peter and Steve, frozen for a moment, look nervously to the source. It's coming from...

ANNIE. Her head is down. She's moaning, as if trying to vomit. She's in some sort of TRANCE. Finally, she lets out a LONG, PAINED GROAN. Guttural and almost inhuman-sounding. It drags out longer than is comfortable to hear. And then...

Annie stops. Her eyes are WIDE. Like a child's. She then says:

ANNIE (CONT'D)

Hello?

But her voice sounds different. It will now remind us — in inflection, in quality — of CHARLIE'S VOICE.

PETER

(horrified)

Mom?

ANNIE

(like Charlie)

Mom?

Annie looks around, as if looking for "Mom." She looks very scared now (but she's *still* squeezing Peter's wrist).

ANNIE (CONT'D)

(like Charlie)

Mom?!

PETER

(to Steve)

I don't like this.

ANNIE (CONT'D)

(like Charlie)

What's happening?!

PETER (CONT'D)

(to Steve)

Dad! I don't like this!

STEVE
(also afraid)
Annie…

ANNIE
(like Charlie)
What's going on?!

Annie is still looking around, as if she can't see. As if she's BLIND.

PETER
(crying)
Mommy?!

Annie is crying now, too.

ANNIE
(like Charlie)
Mom??

Mortified, Peter tugs on Steve's arm.

PETER
Please, Dad!

STEVE
(helpless)
ANNIE! STOP IT!

ANNIE
(like Charlie)
What's happening?! Why is everyone scared?!

Terrified silence.

ANNIE (CONT'D)
(like Charlie)
WHY ARE YOU SCARING ME?!

More terrified silence.

ANNIE (CONT'D)
(like Charlie)
Dad! Peter! I'm scared! Where's Mom?!

PETER
(can't take any more)
DAD!

Steve runs to TURN ON THE LIGHTS. Annie is still possessed, looking blindly about the room.

Steve runs out of the room to go to the KITCHEN.

We stay with Annie and Peter.

ANNIE
(like Charlie)
Peter, what's going on? Where's Mom?

PETER (CONT'D)
Stop it!

ANNIE
(like a scared animal)
Why are you trying to scare me?!

Steve re-enters the room, holding a GLASS OF WATER. He TOSSES it in Annie's face. She GASPS — roused from her trance.

ANNIE (CONT'D)
What the hell! What are you *doing?!*

Annie is frozen. She takes in her drenched body. Max has stopped barking in the other room.

ANNIE (CONT'D)
What just happened?

Peter and Steve are traumatized.

EXT. HOUSE – NIGHT

Steve has pulled Annie outside. He's very aggressive. Annie has wiped the water off her face with a towel. In the b.g., Peter watches from a window.

STEVE
What the fuck did you just do?

ANNIE
I didn't do anything!

STEVE (CONT'D)
I swear to God, Annie —

ANNIE
You were there. You *saw* what happened. That wasn't me!

A fraught beat. Steve stares daggers.

STEVE
What *was* that, Annie?

ANNIE
We communicated with Charlie.

STEVE
(meaning it)
Stop it!

ANNIE (CONT'D)
You *saw* that we did!

STEVE
Did you happen to see your *son* in there? Did you even *notice* that he's absolutely terrified?!

ANNIE
Are you sure *you're* not terrified?

STEVE
I *am* terrified! I'm fuckin' scared of *you.*
(definitively)
Tomorrow. We're going to see Dr. Stetson.

Annie's eyes go cold with recognition.

ANNIE
I don't *wanna* see Dr. Stetson.

STEVE
Well, *I* don't wanna be conducting seances in my fucking living room!

Steve storms inside. Annie follows him. She boils.

ANNIE
Goddamn it! Denial can be a crazy thing, *too*, Steve! To be so *rigid!*

But Steve keeps walking off.

INT. ANNIE & STEVE'S BEDROOM – NIGHT

The moonlight is an icy blue.

Annie and Steve are in bed. Steve is asleep with his back to Annie. Annie is too anxious to sleep.

She turns her face into her pillow, only to notice TWO ANTS crawling on the pillowcase. She looks down to see THREE MORE ANTS on the bed. She then pulls ONE ANT off of her shoulder.

Annie sits up. She looks down to see a TRAIL OF ANTS on the floor, leading into the hallway. The trail is coming from the WINDOW.

Annie gets out of bed and checks the window. It's locked. But the trail seems to be COMING IN through a small gap in the corner of the sill.

Annie follows the trail of black ants out of the room and into the hallway...

INT. HALLWAY – CONTINUOUS

The trail of ants is leading clearly to PETER'S BEDROOM. His door is open. (There is the faint sound of Max's barking, as if heard from a great distance.)

INT. PETER'S BEDROOM – CONTINUOUS

Annie enters Peter's bedroom. The queue of ants continues toward Peter's bed. They crawl up the bed post and onto the mattress, continuing up Peter's leg and across his body — all the way up to his neck.

Annie draws closer. As she approaches, it becomes horribly apparent...

THE BLACK ANTS HAVE COMPLETELY ENVELOPED PETER'S HEAD AND FACE.

PETER (V.O.)
Mom! What are you doing?!

CLOSE-UP OF ANNIE'S FACE. Her expression goes from horrified to confused. She looks up, unnerved, and takes in her surroundings. We cut WIDE to reveal:

Annie is standing in Peter's dark room, but Peter is now sitting up in bed. There are no ants. It was all a dream?

ANNIE
What's going on?

PETER
You were sleepwalking.

There is no audible room tone and the dialogue is strangely CRISP, as though being spoken in a dreamy vacuum. The only other sound is Max's distant BARKING.

Annie looks extremely confused and afraid.

ANNIE
I'm sorry...

Annie looks around.

ANNIE (CONT'D)
Is Charlie here?

PETER
Why are you scared of me?

ANNIE
(looking at him now)
What?

Annie's expression pleads *"How could you ask me that?"* But Peter just stares back at her. Annie's attitude suddenly TURNS — from defensive to confessional. She admits:

ANNIE (CONT'D)
I never wanted to be your mother.

Annie covers her mouth, as if in shock at her own words. She looks to Peter like a child who just accidentally broke something.

PETER
(emotional)
101 Why?

ANNIE
(still covering mouth)
I was scared. I didn't *feel* like a mother. But she pressured me.

PETER
Then why did you *have* me?

ANNIE
It's not my fault...! I tried to stop it.

PETER
How?

ANNIE
(barely able to say it)
... I tried to have a miscarriage.

Peter starts tearing up.

PETER
How?

ANNIE

(also tearing up)

However I could…! I did everything they told me *not* to. But it didn't work. I'm *happy* it didn't work!

Max's muffled barking has become faintly more distinct. Peter is crying hard now.

PETER

You tried to kill me?

Annie, also crying, shakes her head.

ANNIE

I love you.

We cut back to Peter, but his hair and face are now inexplicably DRENCHED in liquid (presumably paint thinner).

PETER

Why did you try to kill me?

We cut back to Annie, revealing that *she's* now drenched in paint thinner, too.

ANNIE

I didn't. I was trying to save you.

We cut to a WIDE TABLEAU of the room. Their silhouettes are in the center, in profile. Behind them a flame IGNITES at a point on the floor. A trail of FIRE quickly blooms in both directions. It spreads quickly (into the shape of a burning triangle), and it concludes its journey at Annie and Peter. Their bodies are instantly SWALLOWED UP by the apocalyptic flames.

MAX'S OFF-SCREEN BARKING HAS NOW BECOME VERY LOUD, VERY PRESENT. It reaches an almost unbearable pitch before we CUT TO:

INT. ANNIE & STEVE'S BEDROOM – NIGHT

ANNIE WAKES UP WITH A START. *It was all a dream.*

Max is barking wildly in the hallway.

A FLY lands on Annie's face. Brushing it away, she notices that Steve's side of the bed is EMPTY. His pillow is also GONE.

INT. WORKSHOP – SAME TIME

A severe work light (beaming down) illuminates the miniature replica of the GRAHAM HOUSE. We PUSH OMINOUSLY IN on the forbidding dollhouse before pushing in on...

The HIGHWAY REPLICA... The replica of Charlie's head is now missing. The blood-smear on the cement marks its absence.

Max's off-screen BARKING persists and continues through the next scene...

INT. PETER'S BEDROOM – SAME TIME

The lights are on. Peter, dressed in his pajamas, sits traumatized on the edge of his bed.

The composition of this shot (wide, high-angle) is MATCHED eerily on the CUT TO:

INT. CLASSROOM – NEXT DAY

Peter sits tensely in the back corner of his classroom.

103 The teacher stands at the blackboard, leading the class through an algebra lesson.

Peter's mind is a storm. He's brought fiercely into the present, however, when a strange, barely perceptible glint of LIGHT (we've seen this before) FLASHES across the room. The light ends at the WINDOW next to Peter.

Peter looks around. Nobody else noticed it. Peter blinks a few times, concerned that he might be seeing things. He turns back to the window to see...

Peter's REFLECTION is staring pointedly back at him.

The color drains from Peter's face. He looks weakly back at his own reflection, whose LIPS CURL into a strained smile..

Overwhelmed, Peter abruptly STANDS UP, distracting the teacher.

TEACHER

Yes, Peter?

PETER

(confused)

I — have to go to the bathroom.

Aware of Peter's recent trauma, the teacher is careful to be extra sensitive.

TEACHER

That's fine. Just take the pass.

Peter leaves, tears welling up.

INT. STEVE'S OFFICE - DAY

Steve sits stiffly at the computer in his office. He has typed into his search engine *"Paranormal evidence, voice channeling,"* but he pauses and then DELETES this. He instead writes *"Symptomatology and management of grief hallucinations."* He presses SEND.

Steve looks over the results, and then clicks on a separate tab. It's a half-composed EMAIL to a fellow psychiatrist. The email reads...

Hi Bob,

I hesitate to write, but I'm worried that Annie might be on the verge of (or in the MIDDLE of)

He's stuck on how to continue.

Steve's cell phone rings. It's an unknown number. He hesitates before answering it.

STEVE

Hello?

There's a strange wave of STATIC and then...

PETER (V.O.)

(almost whispering)

Dad?

STEVE

Peter?

We can hear that Peter is crying, near hysteria.

PETER (V.O.)

Something's at the school.

STEVE

What is?

PETER (V.O.)

It followed me here!

INT. ANNIE'S WORKSHOP – SAME TIME

The cordless PHONE is ringing. Two FLIES crawl across it.

Annie, still wearing her nightgown, nervously works on a FUNERAL HOME model. The ringing STOPS, but then starts again. Annie now turns to ANSWER the phone.

ANNIE

Hello?

Steve is on the other end. We can hear that he is DRIVING.

STEVE (V.O.)

(furious)

Can you guess who just called me from school in complete hysterics?

Annie goes pale.

ANNIE

(gravely)

Charlie?

STEVE (V.O.)

... *What?*

ANNIE

I — nothing. What happened?

STEVE (V.O.)

Peter just called me, Annie. *Terrified.* Crying in the *hall.* He's convinced he's being threatened by some *vengeful spirit.*

ANNIE

Why does he think he's being *threatened?*

STEVE (V.O.)

(no patience)

Listen to me, Annie: I have a son to protect.

ANNIE

What does *that* mean?

STEVE (V.O.)
It means *that's* what I'm worried about right now. *That's* how I'm proceeding.

ANNIE
Don't talk to me like this. He's *my* son, too.

CLICK. He's hung up.

Infuriated, Annie calls Steve back. He answers.

ANNIE (CONT'D)
Don't hang up on me again. I'm not sleepwalking anymore, you understand?

She hangs up.

Annie returns to the miniature funeral home. She carefully (but tensely) presses a freshly GLUED piece of balsa wood against the beautifully rendered wall. She holds it in place.

The phone RINGS. Annie doesn't care. It rings until the ANSWERING MACHINE gets it. After the outgoing message, the machine BEEPS, and a WOMAN leaves a message.

WOMAN (V.O.)
Hi, Annie! It's Margaret at The Asher Gallery. I'm just calling to see how things are with you and your family — I hope everything's okay — and also, just checking in on, uh, how the progress is going. Not that *you* need reminding, but we *are* a little less than nine weeks away, so it would just be nice to get the vaguest sense of where we are. So yeah, call me back whenever, and again, I really hope everything's okay, and our thoughts are all very much with your family, so — okay. Thanks so much.

Click. BEEP.

Annie has grown extremely TENSE over the course of that message. Still applying pressure to the glued-on piece, she pushes a little too hard, and her thumb BREAKS THROUGH the miniature's wall.

Annie FREEZES for a moment, shocked. Then, overcome by sheer frustration, she raises her FIST and SMASHES IT DOWN into the funeral home's roof, SNAPPING it.

Taken by a surge of destructive rage, she SWEEPS the miniature off the table and rises to STOMP her foot through its roof. DESTROYING IT.

Without missing a beat, she grabs a HAMMER and proceeds to SMASH APART the rest of her miniatures. It's a woeful, devastating fit. By the time Annie gets a grip on herself, it's too late. All of the pieces have been destroyed. All except for one... the MINIATURE OF THE GRAHAM HOUSE.

Annie drops the hammer.

INT. FOYER – MOMENTS LATER

Steve and Peter enter through the front door. A bad SMELL immediately hits them.

STEVE

Whoa. Jesus.

They proceed up the stairs. Steve swipes away a fly.

INT. HALLWAY – CONTINUOUS

Peter goes to his room, closing the door behind him.

Steve walks up to the WORKSHOP's door. He opens it without knocking.

STEVE

(entering)

Annie, what is that smell –

But he FREEZES when he sees the state of the demolished room. Annie sits in her chair, completely surrounded by smashed and splintered wood.

STEVE (CONT'D)

(stunned)

...What *happened?*

He looks at Annie and almost immediately understands. *She* did this. His heart breaks.

ANNIE

I didn't wanna look at it anymore.

Steve stares at her for a very long time. He then grabs the PHONE and storms into the hallway, dialing a number.

ANNIE (CONT'D)
(rising)
Hey! Who are you calling?!

INT. ANNIE'S BEDROOM – LATER

Seen through the bedroom window: Steve, downstairs in the living room, opens the front door to greet a pleasant, well scrubbed man (50s). This is DR. STETSON.

DR. STETSON (O.S.)
Hi, Steve.

STEVE
Thanks for coming, Bob.

Annie is watching this from the window overlooking the living room.

STEVE (CONT'D)
Forgive the smell. I think something died in the walls.

Steve gestures, whispering:

STEVE (O.S.) (CONT'D)
She's upstairs right now.

Annie takes this as her cue. She walks defiantly to the stairs.

INT. FOYER / LIVING ROOM – CONTINUOUS

Annie arrives at the bottom of the stairs, confronting Steve and Dr. Stetson in the foyer. Dr. Stetson turns to acknowledge Annie with a big smile.

DR. STETSON
(warmly)
Hi, Annie.

ANNIE
Dr. Stetson.

DR. STETSON
... Can we all sit somewhere and talk?

ANNIE
(disdainful)
Yeah, let's make ourselves at home.

Annie goes to the **LIVING ROOM** and takes a seat at the couch. Dr. Stetson follows to sit opposite her. Steve sits to the side. *(A couple flies will be buzzing throughout the scene.)*

DR. STETSON

How's it going?

ANNIE

Not amazing.

DR. STETSON

Can you talk about why?

ANNIE

(blunt)

Uh — because my daughter was killed and now my psychiatrist husband is calling over his peers to investigate me.

Steve shakes his head to himself.

DR. STETSON

Nobody's investigating you, Annie.

Annie just stares at him.

DR. STETSON (CONT'D)

How are you?

109 ANNIE

I'm *fine*. I'm lucid. I'm in mourning and I'm trying to *cope*, and *he's* supposed to be my partner, so forgive me if I'm not bouncing off the walls to see you.

DR. STETSON

Nobody's trying to do anything against you right now, Annie. I promise you.

ANNIE

Then stop patronizing me, please.

Stetson takes a long pause. He levels with her:

DR. STETSON

What's all this about ghosts? And seances?

ANNIE

(direct)

I thought I felt a presence. I was hopeful, it was fleeting, and now I'm back to grieving.

DR. STETSON

Okay… all right.

(moving on)

And why did you destroy your work?

ANNIE

Because it's my work.

Annie's eyes are stone. Brief pause.

DR. STETSON

(relenting)

Fair enough. So I'm gonna ask you some annoying questions now, Annie.

(making sure to not patronize)

I can *see* that you're lucid.

(first question)

What day is it?

ANNIE

Tuesday.

DR. STETSON

When in the month?

110

LATER

Through the foyer window, we see Steve and Dr. Stetson OUTSIDE. This is from Annie's POV.

Dr. Stetson is explaining something to Steve. Steve nods, frustrated. We see Dr. Stetson say *"I'm sorry, I can't"* and then he walks off to his car. Steve sulks back toward the house.

Steve enters to find Annie standing there.

ANNIE

What were you hoping? That I'd tell your psychiatrist friend that we brought back our dead daughter?

Steve just walks past, going for the stairs.

ANNIE (CONT'D)

(calling after)

You think I'm an idiot?

INT. ANNIE'S WORKSHOP – MOMENTS LATER

Steve has entered the workshop. He walks heavily around the ruins.

Annie steps in. Watches him.

STEVE
You worked so hard for this show.

ANNIE
Jesus Christ — *fuck* the show. You're ignoring this!

STEVE
I'm not ignoring *anything* — *believe* me.

ANNIE (CONT'D)
You ignore *everything!* If you can't find it in one of your books!

Long pause.

STEVE (CONT'D)
(tensely, measuredly)
I won't indulge this behavior anymore.

ANNIE (CONT'D)
"Indulge"?

STEVE (CONT'D)
I *won't.* I can't allow it.

ANNIE (CONT'D)
"Allow" now! Jesus!
(pointing)
You're the one who's gonna go crazy, Steve. If you keep just *denying* what's in front of you.

Steve stares at her, overwhelmed. He looks down to notice at his feet: the figurine of Annie's mother, holding out her breast. Steve lets out a defeated sigh.

STEVE (CONT'D)
(tears building)
You know, Annie... You can still build a shrine to the terrible stuff. Doesn't mean you have to destroy anything good.

ANNIE
Well, it's *not* anything good. It's nothing. It means *nothing. This* —
(kicks a piece of wood)
— is what I cared about.

STEVE

Except for *that* one.

Steve is pointing out the pristine Graham House replica. He looks it over. Something makes him chuckle bitterly to himself.

Annie looks at Steve, not understanding. She walks over to the miniature.

STEVE (CONT'D)

Nice touch.

Annie looks at Steve, not understanding. She walks over to the miniature.

She sees that something has been ADDED to Peter's bedroom. A HEADLESS FIGURINE (now wearing Peter's clothes) is lying in Peter's bed. The color drains from Annie's face.

STEVE (CONT'D)

I was wondering when Peter would get switched with Charlie.

Annie is covering her mouth with her hands. She is having a horrible revelation. Her eyes then SCAN UP to notice something else...

The figurine of ANNIE is now in the ATTIC replica. The figurine is dressed in a NIGHTGOWN (the same one that Annie is wearing now), except its front is covered in blood.

Defeated, Steve leaves the room.

ANNIE

Where are you going?

STEVE

(bitterly)

I didn't sleep at all last night. If you can *believe* it.

INT. LIVING ROOM – MINUTES LATER

Rattled and extremely tense, Steve sits at the couch, which is dressed with a blanket and pillow. He uncaps a PRESCRIPTION BOTTLE (sleeping pills).

STEVE

(mumbling)

Always you — right, Steve? *You* hold it all together.

He draws out TWO PILLS and knocks them back. He then hesitates before pulling out ANOTHER ONE. He DOWNS it.

INT. WORKSHOP – LATER THAT NIGHT

Through the open door of the workshop (whose lights are now off), Peter is seen TURNING OFF THE LIGHTS in his bedroom. He looks out into the hall, paranoid, and then shuts the door. Several FLIES adorn the hallway walls.

This was seen from ANNIE'S POV. She's sitting in the dark, among the wreckage of her work. She's still in shock over the inexplicable additions to the Graham replica.

Suddenly she HEARS the faint sound of a PENCIL VIGOROUSLY SCRATCHING PAPER. It's coming from down the hall. She hesitates before rising and entering the **HALLWAY...**

INT. HALLWAY –CONTINUOUS

More and more flies have collected. They seem especially prominent around the ATTIC DOOR on the ceiling.

Noting this, Annie continues to follow the sound of drawing to arrive at...

INT. CHARLIE'S BEDROOM – CONTINUOUS

The door is open. The lights are OFF. The sound of PENCIL FEVERISHLY SCRATCHING PAPER is heard, although the room is completely empty.

Annie stands at the door. She hesitates before turning on the light.

CHARLIE'S DRAWING PAD rests on Charlie's bed. It's open to a mostly blank page, but a DRAWING IS MATERIALIZING on it. It is then FLIPPED (as if by an invisible finger) to the next page, where a new drawing begins. We can't yet see the content of the drawings.

Annie approaches the drawing pad to investigate. Her eyes, already buzzing with fear, now widen with HORROR.

INT. PETER'S BEDROOM – NIGHT

The door is closed and the lights are off. Peter is in bed, trying to sleep. Silence, save for a buzzing fly. Then...

A CLICKING of the tongue. Peter's eyes OPEN. He slowly looks up, scanning past the bed, to SEE...

CHARLIE is standing in the dark corner of the room. Charlie stares at Peter with unblinking eyes. It's almost too dark to make her out. Another CLICK.

PETER

Charlie?

A long silence. Charlie slowly opens her MOUTH, but then her head DROOPS forward and rolls OFF her shoulders. It tumbles to the floor and rolls toward Peter, but when it rolls into a block of moonlight (cast from the window), it's revealed to be a Nerf basketball.

Peter glares at the ball. A quiet GROWLING is heard from the door. Peter looks up.

The door is now OPEN and Max stands in the doorway. He seems to be disturbed by Peter — or rather, by something standing *behind* Peter.

PETER (CONT'D)

(terrified)

What is it, Max?

Suddenly TWO HANDS materialize from behind Peter's head. They grab his face, grasping under his chin. They TUG BACK on his head, as if trying to yank it off. Peter SCREAMS.

Max runs forward to attack, but the DOOR SLAMS IN HIS FACE. Behind the door: wild barking, followed by a sudden YELP and then the SOUND OF PAWS SCRATCHING AT THE FLOOR. They continue, but swiftly become more and more distant. It sounds like Max is being sucked across the hall by a great, vacuuming force.

INT. LIVING ROOM - SAME TIME

Steve is FAST ASLEEP on the couch.

Off-screen, the sound of Max being TUGGED DOWN THE STAIRS, bumping loudly with each step, and then being dragged across the foyer floor. This is followed by the sound of the FRONT DOOR OPENING and Max being deposited violently out of the house. The door SLAMS SHUT

EXT. GRAHAM HOUSE - SAME TIME.

Max, now outside, paws frantically at the door, desperate to get back inside.

ANNIE (O.S.)

Peter! Peter!

INT. PETER'S BEDROOM – SAME TIME

Peter has just been released by the phantom hands. He's frantic. ANNIE is now standing in the room.

ANNIE

What's wrong, baby?! What happened?!

PETER

What are you *doing?!*

ANNIE

What do you mean?!

PETER

You were pulling on my head!

ANNIE

What?!

Peter looks terrified of her.

ANNIE (CONT'D)

No I wasn't! I just came in! You were screaming!

Peter is crying.

ANNIE (CONT'D)

What happened?

PETER

I saw Charlie in the corner and then you started pulling on my head.

ANNIE

Peter! I would *never* do that to you! Are you *crazy?* I would *never* hurt you. How could you even think that?

Peter just stares at her through frightened tears.

ANNIE (CONT'D)

… You saw Charlie in what corner?

Peter can't answer. He's horrified.

ANNIE (CONT'D)
Listen to me, Peter. I don't know what's happening or what you just saw, but I'm stopping this. Do *NOT* tell Dad what you just said to me. It's *NOT* true. Something's going on, and I'm the only one who can stop this. Do you understand? I'm the only one who can *fix* it.

Peter stares unblinkingly at her.

INT. CHARLIE'S BEDROOM – SAME TIME

Charlie's DRAWING PAD is open. We slowly push in, revealing the CONTENT of two of the drawings...

Both are crude, violently drawn sketches of PETER'S FACE, but the EYES are replaced with X's. The faces are framed by furiously sketched TRIANGLES.

A BREEZE blows in from the window, flipping to the NEXT PAGE — more of the same — and then the next page — still more of the same — and then the next page, etc....

Annie's HAND enters to seize the drawing pad. She leaves the room.

Max's barking persists in the b.g.

INT. LIVING ROOM – NIGHT

Annie has started a FIRE in the fireplace. (In the b.g., Steve is still asleep on the couch.)

Annie clutches Charlie's drawing pad, gazing into the fire. She inhales deeply, holds her breath, and then THROWS the pad in. At first it resists the flames, but then, the EDGE of one sheet begins to BURN.

Annie watches this, eyes glued to the fire. But the shoulder of her SHIRT has sprouted the tiny beginning of a FLAME. It is the same size as the burgeoning flame at the drawing pad's edge. *Annie doesn't even notice.*

The flame spreads slowly along the drawing pad's edge. As this happens, the flame on Annie's shoulder SPREADS ALONG HER ARM. Annie notices this and panics. She desperately tries to stamp out the fire, but it's no use.

The fireplace fire starts to CONSUME the edges of the drawing pad. Simultaneously, ANNIE'S ARM IS ENGULFED FOR A MOMENT IN FLAMES. The fire on her arm is mimicking the fire that's eating the book.

Annie SCREAMS, pulls the drawing pad out of the fire, and STAMPS OUT the flames. As she stamps it out, the fire on her arm is duly EXTINGUISHED.

Annie understands now. *She's tied to the book.*

EXT. GRAHAM HOUSE – NIGHT

The MOON hangs large over the house. We then SLAM CUT to **MORNING.** The moon has been replaced by a shrill SUN.

INT. HALLWAY – MORNING

Peter steps out of his bedroom, backpack slung over his shoulder.

He clearly didn't sleep last night, and his eyes are buzzing with anxiety. He looks down the hall at Annie's bedroom DOOR, which is open by the faintest CRACK. He hesitates and walks off.

Behind Annie's bedroom door: ANNIE stares through the crack, making sure that Peter leaves.

EXT. JOAN'S APARTMENT BUILDING – DAY

Annie, looking frighteningly determined, approaches Joan's apartment building. She's still wearing her nightgown (under a coat).

INT. JOAN'S BUILDING – THIRD FLOOR – MOMENTS LATER

Annie emerges from the elevator onto Joan's floor. She rushes to JOAN'S DOOR and urgently KNOCKS.

No answer.

Annie pauses and then knocks again. And again. And...

INT. JOAN'S APARTMENT – CONTINUOUS

Nobody's home. We are pulling back from the DOOR (as Annie's knocking persists) to REVEAL the apartment...

It looks *mostly* the same, but it's now adorned in cloths and drapes that feature various SYMBOLS. One of these is an ORNATE SIGIL (which we recognize as the one on Annie's necklace). This is the sigil of PAIMON, and it can now be found all over the room.

The TABLE at which Annie and Joan performed the seance (which was then covered in a tablecloth) is now bare, revealing that the table-top has a LARGE TRIANGLE carved into it (pointing to the northwest). Resting in the middle of the triangle is a PHOTO OF PETER. Beside this is an ATHAME (ritual dagger), a scattering of herbs, and *finally...*

A primitive DIORAMA (the same that we saw earlier on Charlie's desk, but now *finished*). Standing center stage is a crude manikin of a human torso whose head is the SEVERED PIGEON HEAD. Atop the head is an aluminum-foil CROWN. Three other sculptures BOW ON THEIR KNEES to the pigeon-headed figure. Their heads are a severed BUNNY HEAD, a severed RAT HEAD, and a severed SQUIRREL HEAD.

Annie's knocking continues.

INT. HALLWAY – CONTINUOUS

Annie ceases knocking. She looks DOWN to notice that she's standing on...

The familiar WELCOME MAT. *"JOANIE."*

Annie's mind starts racing. She thinks for a moment, and then — *it hits her!* Annie RACES back to the elevator.

A SCHOOL BELL RINGS, bridging our CUT TO:

EXT. HIGH SCHOOL – DAY

LUNCH TIME. It's overcast, dark, and windy. Students mill about in flapping clothes.

Just beyond the high school fence is a ROAD with heavy traffic. PETER is seated at an empty table near the fence, eating (or rather, *not* eating) the cafeteria food.

The TRAFFIC NOISE is loud and imposing. Peter LISTENS to it, losing himself in the white noise. But there's something looming underneath the traffic noise...

It's like a distant YELLING, but too distant to make out. Slowly it becomes clearer, more distinct. It's a WOMAN'S VOICE, and it's yelling *"Peter."*

Peter looks up. *Where is it coming from?*

WOMAN'S VOICE
(still vague)
... I expel you...!

Peter looks around. Soon his eyes settle on something...

Across the road, on a far sidewalk, JOAN is standing. She looks raving mad. She's staring *directly* at Peter and she's screaming like a lunatic.

JOAN
SATONY, DEGONY, EPARIGON!

Terrified, Peter rises from his seat. He looks around to see if anyone else is noticing this. Nobody is.

JOAN (CONT'D)
PETER!

Peter looks back at her. They MEET EYES.

JOAN (CONT'D)
GET OUT, PETER!

Peter breaks the gaze. He looks around, appealing to any/all of the circulating kids. It's clear that none of them see or hear this. *How is that possible?*

JOAN (O.S.) (CONT'D)
PETER!!!

INT. GRAHAM HOUSE – UPSTAIRS HALLWAY – DAY

We are viewing the UPSTAIRS HALLWAY in WIDE — in diorama form. It's as if the front walls of the house have been removed. In fact, it looks like ANNIE'S MINIATURE REPLICA, except that it *can't* be, because the hallway is swarming with FLIES (confirming the real-life scale).

Annie, having just returned from Joan's, arrives at the top of the stairs. She runs down the hallway to enter the **WORKSHOP.**

She rushes to the BOXES marked *"Mom's Things."* She opens the first box and finds a HAND-EMBROIDERED WELCOME MAT. *It's the exact same style as Joan's.* Embroidered into it is the name *"ANNIE."* Under that is another mat, bearing the name *"CHARLES"* and featuring the now-familiar sigil of PAIMON.

Annie goes to the next box. She digs through a collection of herbs and oils, and beneath those, she finds a familiar hardback: *NOTES ON SPIRITUALISM.* Below this, a couple of other hardbacks: one that appears to be a GRIMOIRE (book of spells) and the other titled *INVOCATIONS.*

INVOCATIONS' cover features an esoteric sigil. Annie opens the book to find that it's filled with vivid etchings of DEMONIC POSSESSION RITUALS.

Annie goes to a MARKED PAGE. It features an illustration of a beastly man with a hulking body and a strangely effeminate face. He rides a dromedary and wears a crown. Tied to his hip is a collection of SEVERED HEADS. Behind him is a queue of frolicking ghouls, all headless and all playing instruments. A title reads: *"King Paimon (God of Mischief)."*

Annie finds a HIGHLIGHTED PARAGRAPH: *"When successfully invoked, Paimon will possess the most **vulnerable** host. Only when the ritual is **complete** will Paimon be locked into his ordained host. Once locked in, a new ritual is required to **unlock** the possession."*

A sentence underlined in pencil reads: *"Paimon is male, thus covetous of a male human body."*

The next page features an etching of a man sitting atop a mountain of treasure. A caption reads: *"The riches to the conjurer."*

Annie comes to the TITLE PAGE of the book. There is a handwritten NOTE. It reads:

> *My darling, dear, beautiful Annie,*
>
> *Forgive me all the things I could not tell you. Please don't hate me and try not to despair your losses. You will see in the end that they were worth it.*
>
> *Our sacrifice will pale next to the rewards.*
>
> *Love, Mommy*

Mortified, Annie throws the book into the box and digs deeper to find TWO PHOTO ALBUMS, familiarly titled *"Memories."*

Annie flips through one of the albums. For a while, nothing of note. But then she FINDS something...

A PHOTO of ELLEN (Annie's Mother), 20 years younger, standing with JOAN, also 20 years younger. They both wear replicas of Annie's

NECKLACE — the one bearing the now-familiar sigil of Paimon.

Stunned, Annie continues through the photo album. She finds SEVERAL MORE PHOTOS FEATURING JOAN, who's often standing in the background. *Always wearing the necklace.* She and Ellen were evidently close friends.

Another photo: Ellen guides a baby bottle into BABY CHARLIE'S mouth. The bottle's milk is polluted with black herbs.

Finally, Annie comes to a particularly bizarre photo. It features Joan pouring gold/silver coins over Ellen's head. Ellen, wearing a tiara, is weeping/laughing tears of joy. They are surrounded by an intimate, APPLAUDING audience.

INT. HIGH SCHOOL HALLWAY - DAY

Students are returning to class.

Peter walks trembling down the hall. Any lingering kids disperse to enter their classrooms. Peter approaches *his* classroom, a gnawing apprehension taking him over.

Suddenly, from behind Peter, a FLASH of light STREAKS across the length of the hall. It sweeps past Peter. He FREEZES.

The light seems to disappear at Peter's CLASSROOM. Peter stares at the door.

Through the door's window, MR. DAVIES (the teacher) turns to see Peter. They lock eyes. Mr. Davies smiles expectantly.

Feeling pressured, Peter walks to the classroom. He ENTERS.

INT. GRAHAM HOUSE - UPSTAIRS HALLWAY - MOMENTS LATER

The hallway is crawling with flies.

Annie, still holding the photo album, enters (from the workshop) to investigate.

The ceiling's ATTIC HATCH is now covered in more flies than ever. It's clearly the source of the infestation.

Annie, eyes crazed with paranoia, stares at the hatch. A short (but accessible) rope hangs from it, *asking to be pulled.*

Annie pulls on the rope, slowly OPENING the attic hatch and releasing its retractable stairway. A HORDE OF FLIES escapes the attic.

Annie hesitates before climbing up.

INT. ATTIC – CONTINUOUS

The attic is dank and claustrophobic. There is one window, letting in scant daylight. Otherwise, the space is obscured in utter darkness.

Annie pokes her head in. At the foot of the entrance is a FLASHLIGHT. Annie takes it, turns it on, and shines its beam into the shadows.

Flies are everywhere. Their buzzing permeates the room.

Waving away the flies, Annie explores the space. It's filled with discarded pieces of the family's past. Old cribs, a mattress, toys, etc.

Finally, Annie's FLASHLIGHT dawns on something. A FIGURE lying prostrate in the corner. Annie approaches it. The flies get louder. Annie finally gets close enough to SEE...

It is a WOMAN'S CORPSE, and upon closer inspection, its HEAD is seen to be MISSING. From the white and wrinkled hands, it's evident that this was an old woman. She is also wearing a WHITE SILK ROBE — *identical to the one that Charlie saw the corpse wearing earlier in the woods.* (Is this Ellen Leigh's corpse?) A large TRIANGLE has been drawn in chalk around the body.

Annie GASPS, staggers back, and bends over to RETCH. As she does so, the flashlight's beam crosses something on the VAULTED CEILING above the body. Annie pauses before raising the flashlight. She trains it on the ceiling to reveal...

THE SIGIL OF PAIMON has been painted onto the ceiling in now-dry BLOOD. Flies crawl across its coarse black-red strokes.

Outside, it has begun raining.

INT. CLASSROOM – DAY

The sound of rain dancing on the roof and windows.

Peter sits at the back of the class. He WRINGS his hands, anxiety mounting. He's still thinking about the woman (Joan) who was yelling at him.

Mr. Davies stands at the chalkboard. Written on the board: *"Punishment brings wisdom."*

MR. DAVIES
So, everyone feels justified: Iphigenia's murder was commanded by the gods — so really Agamemnon *had* no choice. And Clytemnestra is driven by revenge, just like Orestes when *he* returns...

Suddenly, Peter hears something behind him. A distant CLICKING of the tongue. We focus in on Peter's EAR. Separated by a few seconds each, the clicks become clearer and more present with every CLICK. *It's as if the source is nearing.* Soon it's loud enough to be *RIGHT NEXT TO PETER'S FACE.*

Suddenly, as seen from behind, PETER'S ARM SPIKES UP INTO THE AIR. Because we're behind him, we don't see Peter's face. The tense arm is HELD there, as if being pulled by an unseen force. The clicking sound continues.

Mr. Davies turns to notice Peter.

MR. DAVIES (CONT'D)
(calling on him)
Peter.

Mr. Davies waits, but after a moment, his expression darkens into concern.

MR. DAVIES (CONT'D)
Peter, are you okay?

We now reveal PETER. His face is CONTORTED with terrible stress, as if his head were gripped by an electric vise. His eyes are locked open, his eyeballs darting around, as if appealing for help. His hand remains stiffly raised and he seems to have difficulty breathing. In fact, his face is about to turn purple.

PETER CLICKS HIS TONGUE.

MR. DAVIES (CONT'D)
Peter. What's wrong?

Bridget, staring at Peter, looks especially disturbed.
Peter CLICKS again.

MR. DAVIES (CONT'D)
I...

Suddenly Peter GASPS a horrible, gurgling gasp. It sounds like an agonized SQUEAL, much like the one we heard from Charlie during her allergic attack (before her decapitation).

BRIDGET

(terrified)

Can he breathe?!

A spit-bubble forms on Peter's lips as he struggles hopelessly to speak. But then —

Peter's head is SLAMMED FACE-DOWN into his desk. It holds there, trembling with tension. His face is SMEARED across the desktop, as if a great pressure is being applied to the back of his head. One can almost hear Peter's nose CRUNCHING.

Peter's head suddenly swings back up, as if being YANKED by the hair. He is held upright for a moment, revealing that his eyes are pitch-red with tears. His nose is also bleeding lightly. He looks extremely disoriented.

PETER

MOM!

Peter's head is SLAMMED back down, into the table. Blood BURSTS out of his now-broken nose.

The class screams!

Peter, suddenly in possession of his faculties, KICKS himself back. He stumbles out of his chair, knocking over the desk as he staggers backward. He has been RELEASED from whatever was just gripping him. He SCREAMS, throwing his arms around, fending off whatever it was. He breaks down in SOBS, fraught with terror.

The class is completely silent.

INT. STEVE'S OFFICE – DAY

A haggard Steve sits in his office, nursing a scotch. The dappling window light is distorted by the rain.

His cell phone VIBRATES. It's ANNIE.

Steve just stares at it. Letting it vibrate. It stops.

After a moment, the office phone RINGS. He looks at it. Thinks about answering. Doesn't.

He turns in his chair, raising the scotch to his lips. Ignoring the phone. He downs the glass.

We now reveal the office phone's CALLER ID. This call is coming from Peter's high school.

INT. GRAHAM HOUSE – KITCHEN – DAY

The landline RINGS. It's the high school, now calling the Graham house.

Nobody is home. Max's barking is heard outside.

EXT. GRAHAM HOUSE – SAME TIME

Annie, not wanting to be in the house, is now standing outside. She wears a hooded parka, eyes crazed, standing under the treehouse (shelter from the now-diminishing rain).

She watches the house, gripping her mother's photo album and holding her cell phone at the ready.

ANNIE

(to herself)

125 Goddamn it, Steve! Come home!

Max's barking continues.

INT. STEVE'S OFFICE – SAME TIME

Steve is still in his office, eyes closed, leaning back in his chair. Clinging to the peace. (The rain is settling to a drizzle.)

The phone rings again. He sets his drink on the table and grudgingly answers.

STEVE

Hello?

Pause. Steve suddenly becomes alert.

STEVE (CONT'D)

What? What happened?... What hospital??

INT. CAR (MOVING) – LATE AFTERNOON

Steve is now driving home from the hospital. The rain has stopped and the clouds are opening up.

PETER is asleep in the back seat. His nose is HEAVILY BANDAGED and his eyes are black and blue.

Steve looks at the rearview mirror while he drives. Watches his son sleep.

Steve looks back to the road to see — *he's about to run a red light.* He STOMPS on the brake.

Despite the harsh stop, Peter remains asleep.

Steve grips the wheel, on the edge of his seat. A moment of tense silence, and then: the floodgates open. Steve starts CRYING, overwhelmed. After a moment of this, he regains composure.

The light goes GREEN.

INT. STEVE'S CAR (MOVING) - LATE AFTERNOON

Through the windshield: we're driving up the long Graham driveway. Annie runs into view, bounding toward us. She comes to the driver's side of the car, still holding the photo album —

ANNIE

Steve! Thank God!

— but Steve continues idling toward the house. (He's in no mood for histrionics.) Annie runs alongside the car, but then she notices Peter's BANDAGED NOSE in the back seat.

ANNIE (CONT'D)

Oh my God! What happened?!

Steve parks. He steps out of the car.

ANNIE (CONT'D)

Who did that?!

STEVE

He did apparently. Smashed his own face into his desk, hard enough to break it.

This only feeds Annie's paranoia. She covers her mouth with her hands.

ANNIE

(needing to tell him)

Steve...

But Steve has already opened the back door and is pulling Peter out.

STEVE

(blunt)

Please: just take his feet.

Annie hesitantly gathers Peter's feet. Steve proceeds toward the house, carrying Peter by his underarms.

INT. PETER'S BEDROOM – DAY

Outside, Max's BARKING is heard. It will persist through the following scene.

Steve and Annie lay the comatose Peter into bed. Steve looks down at Peter, sapped. He's avoiding Annie's eyes.

ANNIE

Steve.

Steve waits for her to continue.

ANNIE (CONT'D)

... Upstairs, in the attic... When you were gone, I went up there.

Steve closes his eyes, not wanting to hear whatever's coming.

ANNIE (CONT'D)

There's a decapitated body. An old woman...

Steve's eyes open, numb. He looks blankly at Annie.

ANNIE (CONT'D)

(reacting)

That's what all the flies are!

STEVE

(zero inflection)

A body?

ANNIE

Go upstairs. Look for yourself.

STEVE (CONT'D)

Whose body?

ANNIE (CONT'D)

I think it might be my mother's. I *think!* I can't tell! The skin is black and she's all distended, but it's an old woman and the head is gone... Go see for yourself.

Steve STARES at her before walking into the hall…

INT. HALLWAY – CONTINUOUS

… and approaching the attic hatch.

ANNIE
And then there's more.

STEVE
More than your mother's headless body.
Of course.

Steve reaches for the attic hatch. He pulls it down and a mass of FLIES escapes.

Steve pauses, now much more nervous about what he's about to find. He begins to climb the stairs.

Annie now RUNS downstairs…

INT. LIVING ROOM – CONTINUOUS

Annie rushes to the fireplace. She starts a FIRE.

Max's barking continues off-screen.

INT. UPSTAIRS HALLWAY – MOMENTS LATER

The hatch is still open. We hear from within the attic:

STEVE (O.S.)
Jesus fuck!

Annie has run back upstairs.

Sounds of distress (from above) as Steve rushes to the stairs and stumbles down into the hallway. He's pale with shock.

STEVE (CONT'D)
What the fuck!

ANNIE
There's more.

STEVE (CONT'D)
Why haven't you called the police?!

ANNIE
The police can't help us!

This makes Steve pause. *Did Annie do this?*

STEVE
Who is that, Annie?

Annie squeezes her mother's photo album.

ANNIE
Do you remember Joan, my friend? Her grandson died and she took me to her apartment?

Steve's eyes are narrowed. Something hits him.

STEVE
(to himself)
It did look like your mother.

ANNIE
Listen! She *taught* me how to do the seance. I didn't even *want* to know. But she brought her grandson back, and I *saw* it and I *felt* it — just like *you* did with Charlie.

Steve eyes Annie with growing revulsion. She now opens the photo album. She's frighteningly energetic.

129 ANNIE (CONT'D)
This was my mother's album. Okay? Now look: this woman, right here, *that's* her! *That's* Joan!

Annie is pointing at a photo of Joan (20 years younger) standing with Ellen (20 years younger). Annie speaks quickly to prevent Steve from interrupting.

ANNIE (CONT'D)
She never mentioned knowing my mother and *I* never met her before, but she approached me, she consoled me, and she told me about the seance, she showed me how, and now — look:

Steve can't listen to this, but Annie desperately draws his attention to the photo of Ellen being showered in coins by Joan. Annie points at the NECKLACE.

ANNIE (CONT'D)
That's the necklace my mom gave me. Right? It's my mother's necklace. *Right?*

Now Annie points out another photo: her mother posing with Joan — both wearing the same necklace.

ANNIE (CONT'D)
They're *both* wearing it. And they're wearing it in every photo!

Steve, now completely pale, doesn't react. He's staring at Annie like she's a contagious disease.

ANNIE (CONT'D)
And look at the pattern! Did you see up there? *This* was painted above the body. Right?! In blood?!

STEVE
(dawning on him)
...*You* dug up the grave.

ANNIE
What?!

STEVE
It was *you*, wasn't it? When you were going out, "to the movies"?

ANNIE (CONT'D)
You're not even *listening!*

STEVE (CONT'D)
(horrified)
And when the cemetery called...
(outraged at the thought)
I didn't tell you because I didn't want to *worry* you.

ANNIE
Goddamn it! LISTEN to me, Steve! I know you don't trust me — there's nothing I can do about that — but they put a curse on us, and when we brought back Charlie —

STEVE
We didn't bring back Charlie!

ANNIE
(continuing)
— we made a PACT with something! I don't know what it is, but it's in the house and it wants Peter!

Annie pulls out Charlie's DRAWING PAD. She opens it and flips through the sketches of Peter with his eyes X'd out.

ANNIE (CONT'D)
I watched these pages fill. They're all of Peter.

She looks up at Steve.

ANNIE (CONT'D)
I'm sorry, Steve: I don't know what I did, but Peter's in danger and I'm the one who started this.

Annie takes Steve's arm. He recoils at his wife's touch. She leads him toward the STAIRS.

ANNIE (CONT'D)
If we destroy this book, it'll take me too. I tried to burn it — I tried — but my arm caught fire. On its own. As if I was *linked* to it, because I *am* linked! I *know* that now. But if we *don't* destroy this... Peter will...

She's too overwhelmed to finish her thought. Steve's eyes register no compassion. He skeptically follows her down the stairs.

INT. LIVING ROOM - CONTINUOUS

131 Annie goes down the stairs and urges Steve toward the living room.

ANNIE
I need you to trust me, Steve. It needs to be me. It's my fault!

Annie and Steve have entered the living room.

ANNIE (CONT'D)
I need you to throw it in the fire.

Steve just stares at her.

ANNIE (CONT'D)
I can't do it! I can't throw it in! I'm too scared. But if we don't, it'll be Peter. I know it will.
(breaks down crying at the thought)
It'll be our son!

Annie puts the drawing pad in Steve's hand. She closes his fingers around it. She tries to calm herself down.

ANNIE (CONT'D)
Please, baby. I can't do it. I need you to throw it in the fire.

Annie takes a canister of LIGHTER FLUID from her pocket and proceeds to DOUSE the drawing pad. She then looks at Steve with great love and sadness.

ANNIE (CONT'D)
Even if you can't believe me: you're the love of my life.

Annie KISSES him passionately. It has the desperation of a farewell kiss. Steve's lips are stone.

ANNIE (CONT'D)
I love you, Steve. I love you so much. And I love Peter so much!

Annie is crying hysterically. Max's barking continues.

ANNIE (CONT'D)
Please! Throw it in!

Steve walks in a horrified daze toward the FIREPLACE. But then — he STOPS SHORT. He turns to Annie.

STEVE
I'm not doing this anymore with you, Annie.

ANNIE
(panicked)
What? No.

STEVE
This isn't helping you. You're very sick and I need to call the police.

That does it. Annie storms toward Steve, SEIZES the drawing pad, runs to the fireplace, and HURLS the book into the fire. It is immediately CONSUMED by the flames, and then, like clockwork —

STEVE IGNITES INTO A RAGING BALL OF FLAMES. He cries out as he is instantaneously swallowed up by the screaming fire.

Annie can't even scream. She's frozen in horror. Her eyes are LOCKED on the sight of her husband burning. And what's more, the ominous STREAK OF LIGHT has returned — now bouncing wildly around the room. *Max's off-screen BARKING has reached an insane pitch.*

We see Steve's searing reflection in Annie's fixed pupil. The fire is impossibly violent. Now, at the scene's shrieking apex, the streak of light settles on Annie — *entering her!*

SLAM TO BLACK

Silence.

A distant drumming fades in...

EXT. WOODS - NIGHT

The WOODED AREA behind the Graham house.

A drum circle seems to be in progress somewhere unseen. Repetitive, minimal PERCUSSION (like subdued war drums) thumps faintly and steadily in the distance.

INT. PETER'S BEDROOM - SAME TIME

Silence. Max's barking has STOPPED.

Peter's eyes blink OPEN from his deep sleep. He bolts up with a start. He's in his room, under the covers.

133

He squints with pain. He reaches to touch his nose, but discovers the heavy plaster bandage.

Outside Peter's window: the TREEHOUSE. A dim, golden light — like candlelight — flickers from within.

Peter stares at it. The drums are barely heard in the b.g. They will continue.

The drums are momentarily drowned out by the sound of a SCURRYING OF FEET outside. The motion-censor LIGHTS outside the window are triggered, gently illuminating Peter's walls..

For the briefest moment, in this fleeting light, we see...

ANNIE, still wearing her nightgown, in the top corner of the room. She seems to be FLOATING WEIGHTLESSLY. She's so elevated, in fact, that her head is turned to the side and her cheek pressed against the ceiling. There's something still and composed about her; something resolutely NOT Annie. Her eyes are WIDE and her face expressionless. She's behind Peter, STARING at his back. *He doesn't notice.*

The motion-censor lights SHUT OFF, and the room is obscured *again in darkness.* Annie is no longer visible.

Peter senses something behind him. He pauses, listens. Then he begins to TURN.

Annie, back pressed against the wall, scrambles (in a silent panic) across the wall's surface and OUT the door.

Peter looks back *just* as Annie has left. He didn't see her.

Peter climbs out of bed. He goes to the door...

INT. HALLWAY - CONTINUOUS

Peter enters the dark hallway. Flies are everywhere.

He passes under the ATTIC HATCH — the SOUND OF FLIES is especially aggressive up there — and he walks to his parents' BEDROOM.

He peers in. It's empty.

PETER

Mom? Dad?

A SHARP CLANGING SOUND is suddenly heard from downstairs. Peter freezes. A sustained REVERB fills the house. It sounded like it came from a piano.

Peter remains motionless, listening.

PETER (CONT'D)

Hello?

Peter continues warily down the hall.

He notices that ELLEN'S BEDROOM DOOR IS OPEN. He looks inside. EMPTY.

PETER (CONT'D)

Mom?

Terrified, he closes the door, looks to Charlie's door, which is SHUT, and then proceeds to the workshop. Also empty. He now proceeds to the staircase.

Peter leans to peer down the stairs. He sees nothing. He slowly proceeds downward.

INT. FOYER - CONTINUOUS

Peter arrives at the bottom of the stairs. The foyer is empty.

Peter notices the PIANO, which has crashed to its side. The lid is open and a couple of the wires have been SNAPPED.

Peter carefully walks through the foyer, eyes scanning around. Paranoia building.

He approaches the LIVING ROOM, which is faintly illuminated by an off-screen flame.

INT. LIVING ROOM – CONTINUOUS

Peter stops at the doorway. His eyes travel across the walls to finally come to...

The FIREPLACE. The last of a dim fire (mostly embers) crackles in the pit. And lying before the fireplace is...

A CHARRED, BLACK CORPSE. It lies twisted on the rug.

Peter stands frozen, trying to discern what it is. He takes a reluctant step forward and slowly approaches the dark figure. Peter finally comes close enough to SEE...

The body's HEAD has been violently AMPUTATED. The PINK/RED of the exposed neck contrasts garishly with the crisped whole. The body is on its back, arched and contorted.

Peter looks at the HANDS. The fingers are curled into desperate claws. One finger bears STEVE'S WEDDING RING.

Peter opens his mouth to scream, but all that comes out is a muted gust of air. Tears well in his eyes. He can't even summon the strength to look away. *And above/behind him...*

ANNIE is huddled up into a corner of the ceiling. Her face is twisted with grief and fear, and she is shaking her head — *"no, no, no, no, no"* — as if pleading with the back of Peter's head, like a frightened animal. She holds PIANO WIRE, pulling it taut with both hands. Wringing blood.

Peter FREEZES, sensing something behind him. He slowly turns, *but not toward Annie...*

Peter looks to the *other* corner of the room. The CLOSET DOOR is cracked open. Peter SQUINTS at it. Standing in the dark closet, barely visible, is a COMPLETELY NAKED MAN (60s) — staring at him.

Peter is paralyzed.

He then SENSES something in the corner of the ceiling — where Annie was. His eyes scan tensely to the corner, *but Annie is now GONE.*

Pregnant silence.

Suddenly, from behind Peter, Annie BURSTS SCREAMING out of the darkness, dashing toward him.

Peter RUNS squealing out of the room. He sprints for the STAIRS.

Peter bounds up the staircase, but at the top step, he trips over his own foot. He crashes to his knees, scrambling to get back up. Behind him, we hear Annie pursuing.

Peter races madly through the UPSTAIRS HALLWAY. The attic hatch is now inexplicably OPEN. He dashes for the ATTIC STAIRS.

He runs up the stairs and immediately RETRACTS them — just as Annie reaches him. Peter manages to pull the attic hatch SHUT, *almost* catching Annie's bloody fingers.

INT. ATTIC - CONTINUOUS

Peter LOCKS the floor's hatch. There is a mad POUNDING from beneath.

INT. HALLWAY - CONTINUOUS

Annie is UPSIDE DOWN and straddling the ceiling (as though gravity were no longer a thing). She pulls at the attic knob, SLAMMING her head into the hatch.

She bangs her head crazily against the ceiling, over and over. With every strike, she POUNDS her forehead harder and more wildly against the hatch — like a mad bull, trying to break through by sheer force.

INT. ATTIC - CONTINUOUS

Peter stands in the dark, screaming and crying as the pounding persists. It keeps growing *harder, faster, more insane* — until it STOPS.

Peter listens... Nothing. Just the shrill cacophony of buzzing flies. Beside him, at his feet, is a dwindling BLACK CANDLE.

PETER

(terrified)

Mommy?

Peter looks up. BLACK CANDLES HAVE BEEN SET UP ALL AROUND THE ATTIC. Their flames dimly illuminate the clutter.

Peter now looks to the CORNER that earlier enshrined the headless corpse. The corpse is now gone, but something tiny has replaced it. The distance and weak light preclude Peter from identifying it.

Peter begins to approach the corner, tears streaming. He sees the bloody sigil on the vaulted ceiling above. As he walks, the buzzing gets LOUDER, more concentrated.

Peter continues warily toward the corner, his fear rising. The buzzing has gotten even louder. Finally, Peter gets close enough to SEE...

In the center of the chalk-etched triangle is a PHOTOGRAPH OF PETER WITH HIS EYES X'D OUT.

Stunned and confused, Peter REELS back, knocking over a candle. The corner goes dark. Peter is weeping uncontrollably now. He starts backing away, toward the room's center. His eyes remain glued to his photograph.

PETER (CONT'D)

(to himself, crying)

Please. This isn't happening. You need to wake up.

Peter's teeth are chattering. He's hyperventilating. His trembling silhouette is framed by the WINDOW (and its dreamy moonlight) behind him.

Peter continues backing up, but something makes him FREEZE. A prolonged GROAN, accompanied by the sound of WIRE being wrapped/tightened around FLESH. It's coming from a source about twenty feet away, BEHIND him. This is followed by a swifter, HARSHER SOUND — like a saw being dragged through flesh. A pregnant PAUSE and then the sound REPEATS. A briefer pause and it REPEATS again.

Peter slowly turns around. His eyes travel up to SEE...

ANNIE has somehow gotten in. She floats weightlessly in the air. *(She is faintly illuminated by a candle below her.)* She has looped the PIANO WIRE around her own NECK, which is already straining blood. She TUGS on one end of the wire. It SAWS through her neck. She TUGS on the other end of the wire. It saws even deeper.

PETER (CONT'D)

Mommy!

Annie keeps sawing, FASTER and HARDER and with more ruthless persistence. The sawing sound is horrible. Peter, screaming, TURNS away, only to see:

A MIDDLE-AGED BLOND MAN, completely naked, near Peter. He's SMILING giddily. *(We will recognize him as the man who was smiling at Charlie at Annie's mother's funeral.)* Behind him, two SMILING OLDER WOMEN (also naked). They are crouched together, illuminated by a nearby candle-flame.

PETER SCREAMS, TURNS, AND RUNS STRAIGHT FOR THE WINDOW. HE JUMPS THROUGH THE GLASS.

EXT. GRAHAM HOUSE – CONTINUOUS

Peter has landed face-first into a pile of raked leaves. Small shards of glass are embedded all over his body, but nothing too serious.

Peter lies motionless for a long time.

We cut WIDE to a BIRD'S-EYE VIEW looking down on Peter. He lies face-down in the cold blue moonlight, inanimate. The wind blows softly.

We HOLD on this peaceful, static wide. After a moment, a SHADOW floats gracefully across the ground. It belongs to Annie, who must be above us — *but the shadow seems headless.*

The shadow drifts out of frame, followed by the vague, familiar STREAK OF LIGHT. The light, however, STOPS at Peter. It dances on his back... steadies... disappears into him.

After a moment, Peter's head RISES languidly from the leaves.

His face is marked by a few minor GASHES (from the glass). He looks up, EYES STRANGELY CALM. They even look a bit clouded. He looks ahead to the TREEHOUSE...

PETER'S POV: Annie's floating body has arrived at the treehouse, which is still glowing by candlelight. She ascends into it. For a split-second, before she disappears into the treehouse, we see that ANNIE HAS NO HEAD.

Peter rises to his feet, hollow-eyed. His gaze trained on the treehouse. He seems to be in some sort of TRANCE — *much like the trance that Charlie entered earlier.* After a moment of standing, staring at the treehouse... Peter CLICKS HIS TONGUE.

With that, he begins walking slowly toward the treehouse.

He passes MAX'S DEAD CARCASS, sprawled across a garden.

As Peter nears the treehouse, he looks up to its OPEN WINDOW...

Through the window, from Peter's low-angle POV: a birdcage hangs from the treehouse ceiling. It houses a manic WHIPPOORWILL.

We cut to a WIDE of the treehouse as Peter arrives at the tree's base.

Peter pauses. Looks up. After a beat, he begins to leadenly climb up.

INT. TREEHOUSE – CONTINUOUS

Peter, having scaled the tree, pokes his head through the floor-hatch and climbs in.

The walls are lined with black candles, and before Peter are several MEN AND WOMEN (some elderly, some middle-aged) BOWING on their knees, foreheads against the floor. They are all gathered under a giant SILKY RED CLOAK (resembling a giant red puddle), their heads poking through separate openings.

Standing behind Peter (on the opposite side of the treehouse) is the *terrible object of their reverence.* He turns to see...

A GIANT, 6' WOOD FIGURE MANIKIN. Placed atop its shoulders (in lieu of a head) is CHARLIE'S DECAPITATED HEAD — now in an advanced state of decomposition. The nose is still smashed in, much of the face is black with rot, and it wears a wooden CROWN. One hand grips a wooden SCEPTER (with a wooden hand at its top; its index finger pointed to the northwest). The manikin's other hand is raised to extend its first two fingers and thumb; the third and fourth fingers are bent (like a Christ figure).

Bowing at the foot of the manikin is ANNIE'S HEADLESS TORSO — blood pooling at the neck. Beside her corpse, also prostrate, is ANNIE'S MOTHER'S HEADLESS CORPSE (still dressed in white silk, but in a worse state of decay).

Peter's eyes are WIDE, but still blank. They are FIXED on Charlie's head. He looks more confused than horrified.

Peter turns around to face the groveling, red-cloaked worshippers. They now seem to be bowing in *his* direction.

Among the worshippers is JOAN — her forehead pressed to the floor.

Peter, unnerved, looks away. He notices…

A photo portrait of ANNIE'S MOTHER on the wall. She sits upright and her expression is severe. The frame bears an engraving: *"Queen Leigh."*

We come to a CLOSE-UP of Peter. He looks confused and scared (although not in a way that feels like *Peter*). *We will HOLD on this CU for most of the remainder of the scene.*

The sound of someone RISING. This person (Joan) shuffles past Peter to lift the crown off of Charlie's head. *She is out of focus, but it's clear that she is naked.* She then comes to stand (now off-screen) before Peter. After a moment, the CROWN enters the frame to be placed ceremoniously onto Peter's head.

Peter has TENSED up, desperately avoiding eye contact with Joan. He SENSES something behind him. He looks back (and we pan-tilt) to see…

The headless corpses of Peter's family are now inexplicably bowing in *his* direction.

Peter turns forward again — overwhelmed. He looks trapped. Trembling. His milky eyes are welling with tears.

JOAN (O.S.)
(quietly, trying to soothe)
Hey, hey — no, no — you're all right…

But he is starting to PANIC. His eyes fix fearfully to the floor as his breathing grows erratic. Then:

JOAN (O.S.) (CONT'D)
Hey, *hey: Charlie.*

Peter's breathing HALTS. He looks up to Joan, still trembling. Eyes wide.

JOAN (CONT'D)
You're all right now.

A long silence as Peter searches Joan's face for understanding. Then:

JOAN (O.S.) (CONT'D)
You are Paimon. One of the eight Kings of Hell.

Beat. Peter doesn't react. He just stares at her, uncomprehending.

JOAN (O.S.) (CONT'D)
We have looked to the northwest and called you in. We've corrected your first body and give you now this healthy male host. We reject the Trinity and pray devoutly to *you*, great Paimon: give us your knowledge of all secret things and all mysteries of the Earth; bring us honor, wealth, and good familiars; and bind all men to our Will, as we have bound ourselves for now and ever to Yours.

We hear Joan return to her bowing position:

JOAN (O.S.) (CONT'D)
Hail Paimon.

Peter's eyes are buzzing.

Then, from behind Joan:

WORSHIPPERS (O.S.)
Hail Paimon!

141 Then, louder:

JOAN/WORSHIPPERS (O.S.)
Hail Paimon!!

EXT. TREEHOUSE – CONTINUOUS

WIDE of the treehouse.

WORSHIPPERS (O.S.)
Hail!!

CUT HARD TO **BLACK.**

HOLD ON THE BLACK.

From this, we **VERY SLOWLY FADE IN ON:**

A NEUTRAL WIDE OF THE GRAHAM HOUSE. NIGHT.
A strong artifice distinguishes the image. As if the actual house has somehow been replaced by its MINIATURE REPLICA. Even the surrounding trees and flora, dancing artificially in the wind, look FALSE.

Hold on this as the CREDITS roll.

SECTION II

24 FRAMES

CINEMATOGRAPHY BY PAWEL POGORZELSKI

00:01:53

00:10:15

00:13:07

00:19:32

00:24:30

00:25:06

00:29:19

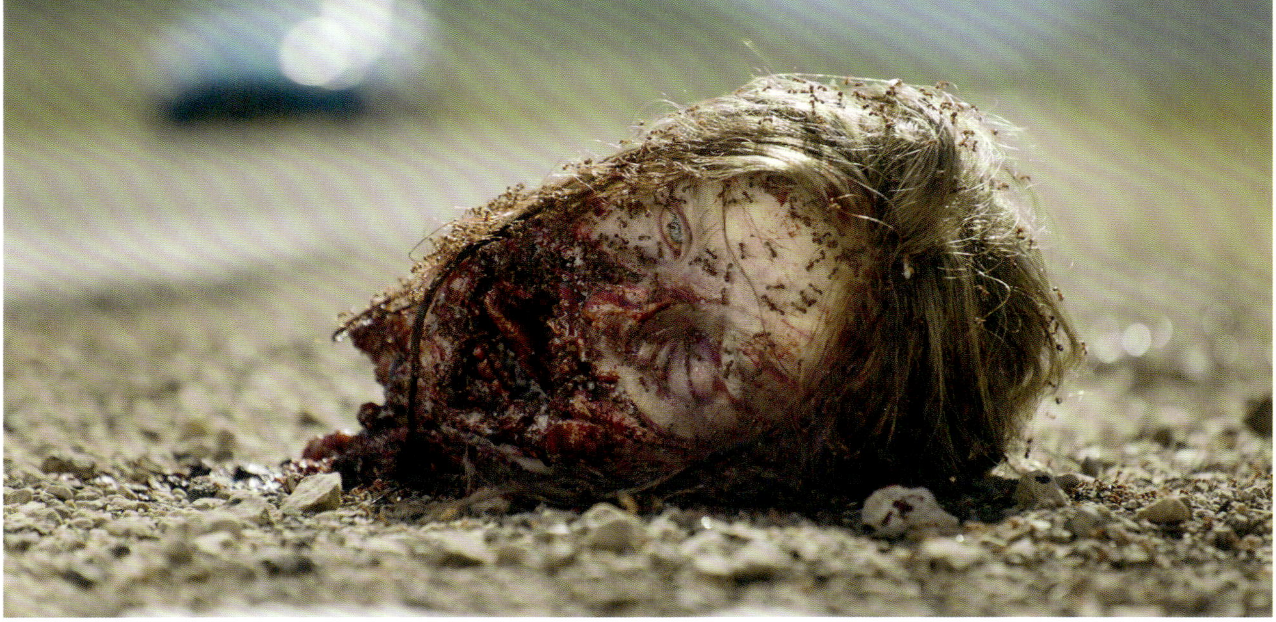

00:37:40

00:40:56

00:41:40

00:52:13

00:58:05

01:00:35

01:12:40

01:31:40

01:32:43

01:38:16

01:46:39

01:46:55

01:48:25

01:53:33

01:55:59

01:59:34

02:02:50

LOVE AND TERROR

BY LESLIE JAMISON

The dollhouse bedroom appears for only a moment: a young woman nursing her infant daughter in bed, while her silver-haired mother stands above them, baring one wrinkled breast through her open nightgown. Let me feed her, too. Let me feed her instead.

This miniature takes something good and familiar — the primal bond between baby and breast — and makes it the site of something dark, imposing, sinister: the breast where it doesn't belong, the mother who can't stop mothering, the prospect of forcing the aging breast into the tiny young mouth, the maternal love that is somehow too much.

I have come to suspect that everyone has a horror movie perfectly tailored to the contours of her psyche, like a jigsaw puzzle piece: a film uniquely positioned to frighten her more than any other. This film takes whatever she trusts most fully in this world — what she relies on most fully, has the deepest faith in — and darkens it, or reveals what has been dark inside it all along. The haunted house as darkened home. Possession as darkened beloved. Devil as darkened God.

My deepest faith has always attached itself to maternal love: my mother's love for me, and then my own love for my daughter. Everything else in the world might dissolve or break, but these bonds have always promised to lie beyond the possibility of rupturing.

One of my strongest childhood memories is an image from my grandmother's house, a chocolate-brown bungalow with sage bushes shadowing the front stoop, and tomato plants in the back garden. Between the living room and the dining room, there was a floor heater that felt like the nerve center of the house: a metal grating that sent up gusts of warm air, and got so hot it could burn the soles of your feet. I can remember the sight of my grandmother and my mother standing on it, side by side, their long billowing skirts filling with its heat like sails catching wind. They were like gods, powered by some secret force below the earth.

I have come to suspect that everyone has a horror movie perfectly tailored to the contours of her psyche, like a jigsaw puzzle piece: a film uniquely positioned to frighten her more than any other.

I watched *Hereditary* in a hotel room in St. Paul while I was on a book tour. My toddler daughter was with her father back in Brooklyn. The film begins with a mother's death, which is actually a feint — it's not really about her absence, but about her terrible, abiding presence. The plot finally makes its way to her corpse: it's been in the attic the whole time, headless and rotting, circled by candles, swarming with flies. Her daughter thought she was gone, but in truth she's been there all along —

festering inside the place they call home, an infection trapped under the skin. Like an aging breast foisted upon a tiny baby, the mother's body in the attic is too much, the wrong kind of presence: the mother who won't go away, won't put away her milk, won't put away her death. Her betrayal is twofold and contradictory: she is gone, but too much of her remains.

We often say: My mom has always been there for me. Or at least I say it. She came into my bedroom when I cried in the night. She flew across the country when I was starving myself. She stayed for months after my daughter was born, to bring me clinking glasses of ice water as I nursed, to help me find the first tiny fingernail I clipped — that minuscule moon, fallen to the carpet — because I wanted to save it forever, like a talisman.

Once I had my own baby, I needed my mother as if I were a baby again. And when she left, I wept like an infant, inconsolable, because the whole world was ending.

In my Minnesota hotel room, I had to pause the movie at the sight of the mother's corpse under its cloud of flies. It was too much, all that buzzing. It was too alive. It was infectious. It claimed too much of me.

When a woman finds her dead mother in the attic, or hears her dead daughter in the back seat of her car, it's as if the film is telling me, Our mothers live inside us, and our daughters live inside us. We have no choice. This is the dark contract of our love for them, and their love for us. We'll never be free of them. A grandmother "gets her claws" into her granddaughter when she gives her a bottle of milk mixed with demon herbs. After a mother is possessed by the malicious ghost of her dead daughter, she tries to burn the sketchbook that summoned her spirit, to sever the link for good, but it's her own arm that catches fire instead. And when her arm bursts into flame, it's as if that sacred subterranean force beneath my grandmother's floor heater — the one that billowed her skirt full of heat, and my mother's beside her — has turned into something sinister. Now it's setting the world on fire. No mother's body is free.

After I paused the film, I saw a text from my daughter's father. She'd climbed out of her crib and fallen to the floor. In an instant, I felt the thousand miles between us. She'd been crying, he said, and maybe a little embarrassed, as if she had done something wrong. I should have been there, I thought. I should have been there to tell her she didn't do anything wrong. Anytime she was hurt and I wasn't there, it felt like I'd done something wrong.

The impossible love: Too present. Not present enough.

The most terrifying scene in the film isn't the headless body of the grandmother, or the headless body of the daughter. It's not the ghost in the corner, the father on fire, or the mother dangling from the rafters. It's the mother wailing in her bedroom after her daughter dies. She is prostrate on the wooden floor, beside the same bed where she nursed her as an infant years before. It looks like she's praying. There is something holy about loving someone so much you can't recover from losing them. There is something sacred and terrifying about the possibility of being utterly destroyed by attachment.

This is the most frightening thing I could imagine — a love so strong it overwhelms me utterly — and I don't have to imagine it. It's a cold glass of water and a fingernail the size of an apple seed. It brings me to my knees. It lives under the skin. Right where she was. Right where I was. Where we remain.

LESLIE JAMISON is a novelist, essayist, and professor. She is the author of the essay collections *Make It Scream, Make It Burn* and *The Empathy Exams;* the memoir *The Recovering;* and the novel *The Gin Closet.*

SECTION IV

FAMILY SEANCE SHOT LIST

BY ARI ASTER

I started composing shot lists before it occurred to me to draw storyboards. Happily, these resulted in movies, more or less, so I committed to this method and haven't deviated. The crew typically finds these shot lists to be largely incomprehensible, so it's become a tradition to go scene-by-scene through the entire document with my cinematographer Pawel Pogorzelski and my production designer (in *Hereditary*'s case, the wonderful Grace Yun) during pre-production. This can take many weeks, usually months, as I struggle to illustrate what I'm pretty sure I meant by my shot descriptions (which vary in clarity, depending on the states in which they were written) by sketching out the proposed blocking of actors and camera positions on whiteboards — like game plans. This is especially necessary when the budget is tight and elaborate sets must be built. (It's best to know which set walls need to be removable *before* you build. And why invest thought, resources, and time into a corner of a room that ultimately won't be filmed?) The obvious argument against all this is: What if you want to play around and improvise on set, encourage spontaneity, and allow for the possibility of finding something better "on the day"? I've heard it all.

I'm often confused by these shot lists, forgetting what I meant by an awkwardly worded sentence — sometimes wondering whether I meant "left" when I wrote "right." When writing them, I often spend thirty minutes agonizing over how to describe a shot that could have easily been drawn in thirty seconds. Even the self-deprecating attitude of this intro isn't to be trusted, as I clearly have enough of my ego invested in this method to allow/encourage the publication of a process that I pretend to devalue.

Anyway, here's a cautionary example.

1.

CU — the "stacked houses" miniature. We are BOOMING UP from the bottom of the miniature, scanning upward across the three buried dollhouses as we hear Annie coming down the stairs. Begin TRACKING LEFT at a diagonal (still booming up) to start including the stairs to the right; soon the top of the miniature is in the FG and the staircase in the MG. Annie's feet walk down in medium, followed by Steve and Peter. We PAN RIGHT with them, allowing Steve and Peter to stop at the foot of the stairs (Annie has hurried to the dining room in the BG). Steve and Peter walk forward, and **we TRACK after them, following their backs toward the dining room,** where the lights are off and the candle has been lit on the table. Annie is at the table, and Steve and Peter STOP at the doorway. We continue tracking to Steve's left side, **PANNING right to become a profile CU of Steve.** Steve says "It's freezing" and goes for the window. We **TRACK LEFT** with him (passing Peter) as he walks toward the window, arriving at **Annie's shoulder in the FG (looking toward Steve; she's at the dining table)** as she yells at him to stop (when he's midway across the room). She sits down; **we BOOM DOWN with her sitting,** remaining an **over-Annie's-shoulder of Steve.** They argue, and when it's clear that Steve won't sit, Annie says "Fine!" and stands up. She stands up in front of the camera, her torso filling the frame for a moment. (This is a cutting point for us to go from this shot to the next. The next portion of this shot is a different shot [1A] pretending to be a continuation of the first shot.)

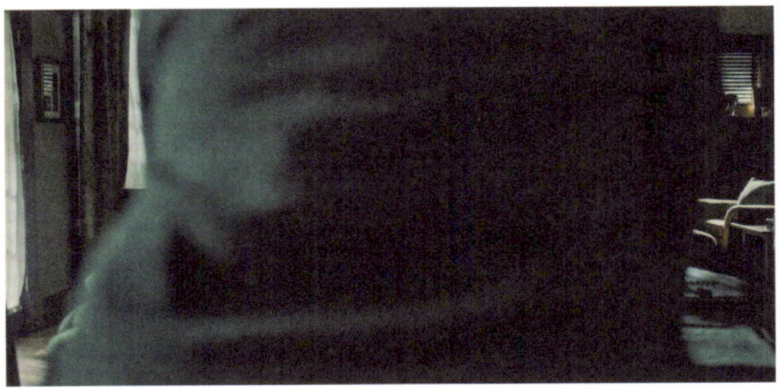

1A.

A continuation of the last shot.

Annie, having just stood up, is filling the frame with her back. Annie steps forward, **becoming a medium of Annie at the table.** She drags the table toward Peter (to the right and at an outward diagonal) and we **TRACK RIGHT with her to arrive at a medium of Annie and Peter at the table (with table in the FG).** Annie goes to Steve in the BG, grabs his hand, and pulls him toward the table. **We now have a three-shot of Steve (frame left), Annie (center), and Peter (frame right).** Right as Annie arrives with Steve, we begin a **VERY subtle PUSH-IN to become a medium CU of Steve and Annie** as she urges him to concentrate. When she yells "Fuck! I'm a medium," we STOP pushing in. When Steve tells Peter to "Go to bed," Annie turns to Peter, and **we PAN RIGHT with Annie's turn to become a medium CU of Annie and Peter.** When Peter tells Steve that he'll stay, **Annie turns back to Steve ("Please, Steve") and we PAN LEFT with her to become a medium CU (again) of Annie and Steve.** Hidden in the pan, we've now begun **PULLING BACK OUT from this (to become a loose medium) of Annie squeezing onto *both* their hands, BOOMING SUBTLY DOWN to include Joan's page in the FG** (by the time she says "Okay, good. I already read that earlier"). Annie gets them to concentrate and then calls out to Charlie.

2. Omitted

3.

Tight medium CU — Steve (camera to the right of Steve, basically mid-table). Reacting to Annie as she calls out to Charlie ("Charlie, are you here?"). We then **pan right** from Steve (looking at Annie) to a **straight-on CU of Annie** as she continues speaking to Charlie. "Charlie, it's Mommy and Daddy and Peter." After this, the creaking is heard, and *we cut away to **shot 4,*** and then we come back to this shot for Annie saying "Charlie, if you're here, I'm going to have us all touch this glass." She takes Peter's and Steve's hands, and **we TILT DOWN as she puts their hands on top of the glass,** and in the tilt we hide a **PULL BACK/ BOOM UP to become a HIGH-ANGLE MEDIUM of them.** Annie calls upward to Charlie. This lasts until Peter feels the pulsing in the air. He TENSES up. "What the hell?" "What's wrong?"

Shoot at same time as 5.

4.

To be inserted in the middle of shot 3.

CU of Peter (at a slight angle, to the right of him). He reacts to the creaking behind him, turning to look over his left shoulder. **We TRACK SWIFTLY FORWARD (and slightly at a right diagonal) with the turn of his head, PANNING almost 180 degrees to stay with Peter's face. We arrive at a medium CU *behind* Peter,** who is now looking directly past us. He then turns back.

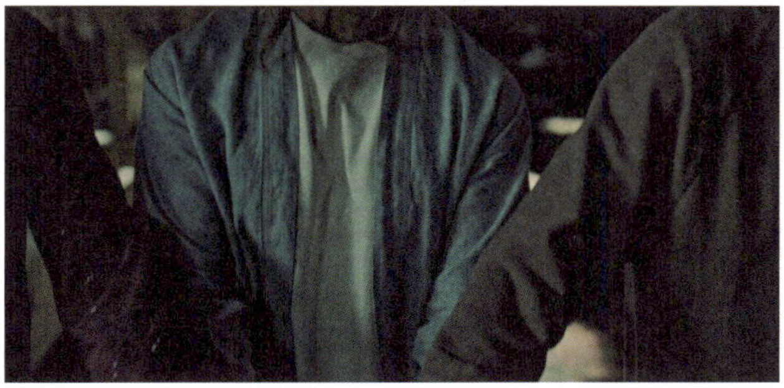
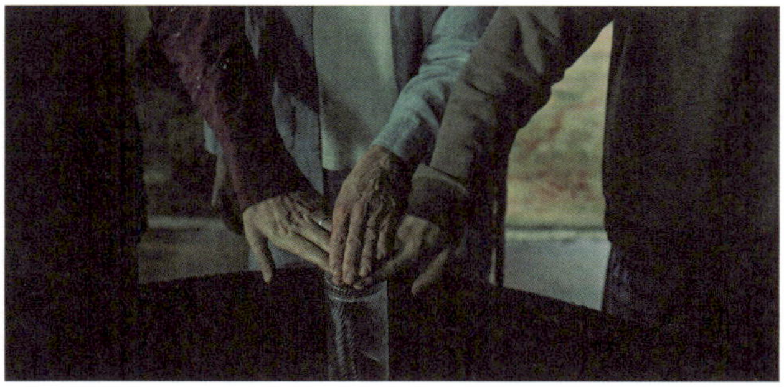

5.

Cut to this after the end of shot 3.

CU profile (camera on Peter's left side) — Peter TENSING up. He says "What the hell?" and then we **RACK focus** to Steve in the BG, becoming an **over-Peter's-shoulder MEDIUM CU of Steve.** We **rack focus back to Peter as he says "like a flexing in the air."** *(Do we start this with the focus on Steve? Perhaps it makes more sense to cut to this shot right after Peter says "What the hell?" in the last shot.)*

Shoot at same time as 3.

6.

CU — the glass (just above level with the table). It MOVES toward us (the hands are retracted!) and **we PULL BACK as the glass continues swiftly toward us (keeping it the same size in the frame). We continue pulling back, TILTING UP to become a medium three-shot of the family (slightly low angle, focus racked to them) with glass in the FG.** Steve and Peter look shell-shocked (cut to 7 and 8) as Annie flips open the drawing pad to an empty page.

7.

Slightly low-angle CU — Steve, staring at glass that moved.

Shoot at same time as 8.

8.

Slightly low-angle CU — Peter, staring at glass that moved.

Shoot at same time as 7.

9.

Medium wide semi-profile — to the table's right, very slightly low angle (Peter nearest, Annie in the center, Steve farthest) — Annie leans across the table to pull the drawing pad toward her. She flips to a blank page and puts a pencil on top. When she reaches across the table, **this motivates us to begin revolving to the left around the table.** We continue to revolve around the table, arriving at the opposite side of the table **(now nearing semi-profile of Steve's shoulder in FG, Annie in center, and Peter in BG)** when Annie shows Steve the drawing of the car. **Before we can settle at the end of the track, we begin PUSHING IN VERY GENTLY toward Annie and Peter.** When Annie returns the pad to the table, **we TILT DOWN with the pad and then TILT STRAIGHT BACK UP to the three of them.** Annie then GRABS their hands, and **we TILT DOWN AGAIN to the table as she presses the hands down.** They pull their hands away, and **we TILT BACK UP as Annie SEIZES Peter's hand.** We are **continuing to push into a medium CU of Annie and Peter (moving past Steve's shoulder)** as she tells Peter not to be scared, then calls out "Charlie? Are you finished with the drawing?" THEN —

10.

Medium of the CUPBOARD DOOR SLAMMING SHUT, and we PAN SHARPLY to Peter's and Annie's and Steve's backs, looking over their shoulders. Peter screams "Mom?!"

11.

Slightly low medium wide — the family (Annie centered). "Charlie? What's wrong?" Then the FLAME BELCHES and is extinguished. Semi-darkness (and Max barking), and a moment later, the flame is **reignited.** Steve bends to look under the table.

12.

Tight medium profile (from the right side of the table), UNDER THE TABLE — Steve looking under the table. He suddenly hears a **moaning** and we **BOOM UP with Steve as he rises back up.** He looks to **Annie (in the FG)** to see that she's the one moaning. Hold on this through the rest of Annie's possession. When Steve runs to turn on the lights, we **PAN to follow him out of the room.**

13.

Slightly low CU — Annie. Eyes closed, head down, finishing her moaning. THEN — she looks up, eyes like a child. "Hello?" Hold on this through the rest of the scene. Continue holding on this as the lights are turned on and then stay on this until water is thrown on her face and she is roused from her trance.

Shoot at same time as 15.

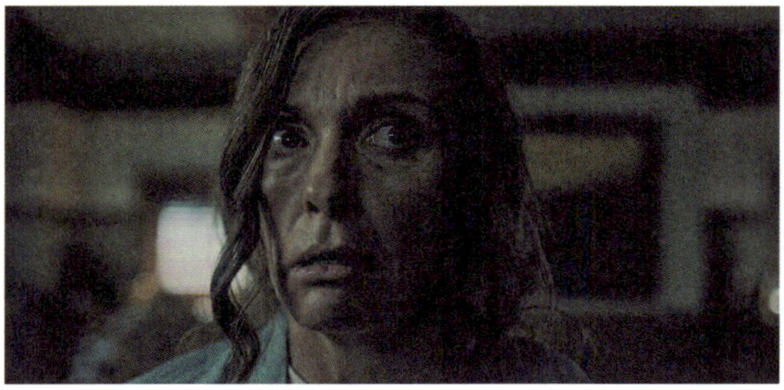

14.

CU — Steve. Hold on this through the possession, until he runs out.

15.

CU — Peter.

Shoot at same time as 13.

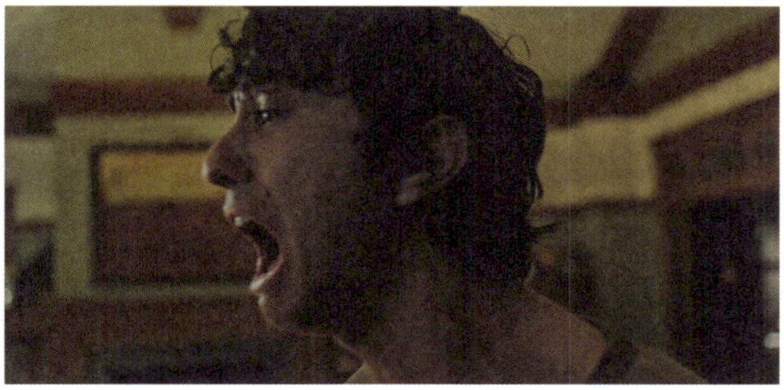

16.

Two shot of Annie and Peter alone at the table after Steve leaves (favoring Peter, both of them semi-profile). The door to the TV room in the BG. Steve runs in from the BG with a glass of water. He runs toward us and throws the water in her face. She GASPS.

Shoot at same time as 17.

17.

Medium of Annie, over Peter's shoulder. Steve runs in, throws water.

Shoot at same time as 16.

"HEREDITARY"

WRITTEN AND DIRECTED BY
Ari Aster

A24
PalmStar Media
PRESENT

a Kevin Frakes
and Lars Knudsen
PRODUCTION

IN ASSOCIATION WITH
Finch Entertainment
and Windy Hill
Pictures

EXECUTIVE PRODUCERS
Ryan Kreston
and Jonathan Gardner

CASTING BY
Jessica Kelly

PRODUCTION DESIGNER
Grace Yun

COSTUME DESIGNER
Olga Mill

MUSIC BY
Colin Stetson

PRODUCED BY
Kevin Frakes, p.g.a.

PRODUCED BY
Lars Knudsen, p.g.a.

PRODUCER
Buddy Patrick

EXECUTIVE PRODUCERS
Toni Collette
and Gabriel Byrne

DIRECTOR OF PHOTOGRAPHY
Pawel Pogorzelski

EDITORS
Jennifer Lame
and Lucian Johnston

MUSIC SUPERVISOR
Joe Rudge

ASSOCIATE PRODUCERS
Beau Ferris
Tyler Campellone
Brandon Tamburri
Jeffrey Penman

CAST (IN ORDER OF APPEARANCE)

Peter..ALEX WOLFF
Steve...GABRIEL BYRNE
Annie..TONI COLLETTE
Charlie......................................MILLY SHAPIRO
Bridget...................................MALLORY BECHTEL
Joan...ANN DOWD
Charlie's Teacher...................CHRISTY SUMMERHAYS
Mr. Davies....................................MORGAN LUND
Brendan...JAKE BROWN
Student #1..............................HARRISON NELL
Student #2..............................BRIANN RACHELE
Spanish-Speaking Woman.................HEIDI MENDEZ
Translator..................................MOISES TOVAR
Group Leader..........................JARROD PHILLIPS
Aaron......................................BROCK MCKINNEY
Boy In Room...........................ZACHARY ARTHUR
Man At Wake.............................DAVID STANLEY
History Teacher...................................BUS RILEY
Stoner #1.................................AUSTIN GRANT
Stoner #2...................................GABE ECKERT
Stunt Coordinator......................ELIZA COLEMAN
Stunts.......................................PETER EPSTEIN

....WHITNEY COLEMAN
....MARK CHADWICK
....CORBETT MCALLISTER
....JENNIFER LAMB
....BRETT SMRZ
....ROCKEY DICKEY
....MICHAEL MCGUIRE
....NICHOLES ANTONIO
....MATTHEW BELLOWS

CREWS

Executive Producer.................................WILLIAM KAY
Line Producer / UPM.........................SCOTT E. CHESTER
First Assistant Director..........................DAVY LEEMAN
Second Assistant Director......................MATT PUNOSEVIC
Second Second Assistant Director............MARSCHELLE WALKER
Art Director...................................RICHARD OLSON
Assistant Art Director........................DEBBIE WHEATLEY
Art Department Coordinator........................ASHLEY COOK
Graphic Designer...................................LOREN KANE
Storyboard Artist...............................JONATHAN HALLETT
Art Department Production Assistant.............CASEY WALKER
Camera Operator................................BRIAN SULLIVAN
"A" Camera First Assistant.........................ANDY BAKER
"A" Camera Second Assistant.......................MATT LESLIE
"B" Camera First Assistants.....................JASON PAINTER
....ERIN NAIFEH
"B" Camera Second Assistants...................KODY RIEKENA
....AUSTIN GREEN
Steadicam Operator...................................JED SEUS
Jib Operators...................................STEVE HOLMES
....KIM HOLMES
Digital Imaging Technicians.........................((RADAR))
....DAREN SMITH
....LISA KONECNY
Stills Photographer...............................REID CHAVIS
Camera Production Assistant.....................RYAN CLINTON
Production Sound Mixer..........................STEVE LANERI
Boom Operators.................................JOSEPH GARRARD
....RYAN PEDERSEN
Gaffer..JASON ROGERS
Best Boy Electric..............................TIM REYNOLDS
Electricians......................................CALEB RASAK
....AUSTIN MURPHY
....WALLACE COX
Key Grip.......................................CRAIG SULLIVAN
Dolly Grips.......................................GLADE QUINN
....RICK MAXEY
....TYLER FURNER
Best Boy Grip.......................................K.C. OLSEN
Grips...ALEX STEIN
....JASON WALSER
....AMBYR REYES
....JEFF ROSENBLATT
....CRAIG KATAYAMA
Chapman Hydrascope Technicians......................IAN CURRY
....ERNEST RYDBERG
Additional Lamp Operators.......................WILLIAM LONG
....JAMES BROWN
....MISO TUNKS

Special Effects Coordinator........................RYAN ROUNDY
Special Effects Foreman...........................MIKE ROUNDY
Special Effects Assistants.........................MATT HALL
....BROCK GOUETT
Special Effects Technicians...................CHARLES ROUNDY
....CURTIS DECKER
Laser Effects.................MIKE GOULD, ILLUMINATUS LASERS
Set Decorator....................................BRIAN LIVES
Leadman..JASON HAASE
Buyer..CYNTHIA NEIBAUR
Swings...CODY FAIRBANKS
....STUART LAKE
....ROCKY JACKSON
On-Set Dressers.................................SHANE ETSITTY
....ERIC BILLY
Property Masters................................SCOTT ARNEMAN
....WRAY FEATHERSTONE
Assistant Property Masters.....................CHASE COLEMAN
....SCOTT SCHMIDT
Property Maker.....................................SAM DEMKE
Property Production Assistant...................ETHAN HAMME
Assistant Costume Designer...................HEATHER GAITHER
Wardrobe Supervisor.............................AARON SWENSON
Set Costumer.......................................COVEY QUIST
Additional Costumers..........................CRYSTAL PUCKETT
....NATALIE PASCUAL
Costume Production Assistant......................EMMA SNOW
Makeup Department Head.............................GREG MOON
Key Makeup Artist..............................ABIGAIL STEELE
Additional Makeup Artist........................SHALYSE LOPEZ
Makeup Prosthetics...............................CHRIS HANSON
Hair Department Head..................ROCKETS "LORA" LAING
Key Hair Stylist................................BOBBI MURPHY
Additional Hair Stylists.........................MEGAN DANNER
....LINDEY CROW
Prosthetic and Miniature Effects By.............APPLIED ARTS
....FX STUDIO, INC
Project Supervisor..............................STEVE NEWBURN
Key Effects Artists..............................KAYLA DOBILAS
....ADRIAN STANSFIELD
....NEIL MORRILL
....JAIMIE CRADDOCK
....JESSICA CRADDOCK
....LINDI CROW
Additional Makeup Effects and Prosthetics........CHRIS HANSON
Construction Coordinator.......................JOHN MALMBORG
Carpenters..................................JOHNATHAN ERICKSON
....WILLIAM DOUGHERTY
....KEVIN JONES
....CHRESTEN POPE
....JOHNATHAN GRIFFITH
....MARK COLLOTON
....ROBERT C. APPERSEN
....MATTHEW SNOW
....ADAM JACKSON
....MATIAS ALVAREZ
....JOHNNY SHEPHERD
....TIMOTHY HOHN
....GARY GRIFFITH
....WAYLON HUFFMAN
Key Scenic.....................................DAVID BROTHERS
Scenics......................................ROSEMARY HILLYARD
....RICHARD PENROD

....JOSIE FIFE
....MEGAN BRANSON
Key Greensman..........................GABE JESSOP
Greens Foreman........................SCOTT RULEY
Transportation Coordinator.................BRITANI ALEXANDER
Transportation Captain......................PAUL LOWELL
Cast Driver..............................MELANIE OLMSTEAD
Van Drivers..............................CHRISTOPHER EDGAR
....ALLEN CAPPS
....DALLIN BASSETT
....APRIL HANSON
Honeywagon...............................JACOB THOMAS
Stakebed Wardobe..........................NICK LARSON
Stakebed Makeup...........................PATRICK SMITH
Fueler...................................SAM PAPPAS
Camera 5 Ton..............................CHAD THOMPSON
Grip 10 Ton...................................MIKE LAW
Electric Truck............................EARNEST HAUFF
Truck Driver..............................ROB TURNER
Drivers.......................................ROB MENG
....RICK SPIDELL
Location Manager..........................ANDREW HODGE
Assistant Location Manager.....................JOE DAY
Location Scout............................ANDY LANGTON
Script Supervisors........................BRIANNA WALL
....LEX HOGAN
Production Coordinator.....................NATANIA GARRETT
Assistant Production Coordinator..............SAMANTHA COOK
Production Secretary.......................ETHAN PAUR
Office Production Assistants.................MELISSA DEARR
....JAMES GILLETTE
Production Accountant......................JENNIFER RICCI
Second Assistant Accountant..................JACK DIAMOND
Payroll Accountant........................KATHLEEN DOMBO
Head Wrangler.............................FENTON QUINN
Wrangler.................................JOYCE QUINN
Animal Wrangler, Ants......................JEREMY WESTERMAN
Animal Wrangler...........................ROGER BLOMQUIST
Casting Associate..........................REBECCA DEALY
Utah Casting..............................JEFF JOHNSON
Extras Casting............................GAYLE MINKEVITCH
Key Set Production Assistant.................AARON EKLAND
Set Production Assistants...................AUSTIN CUMMINGS
....JANZEN VERTNER
....EVAN LAI-HIPP
....ERICA ELMER
...................................MERCEDES WILLIAMSON
Assistant to Mr. Chester....................CAMERON THUMAN
Stand-Ins................................BRETT PENDLETON
....CHAD WRIGHT
....ANGELLA BENNETT
....BRIAN ANDERSON
Catering..................................SMALL POTATOES
....ROB BOLDT
Catering Assistant.........................DYLAN BOLDT
Craft Service..............................MATT SERNA
Craft Service Assistant......................DANIEL MARTINEZ
Set Medic.................................JEFF MIDGLEY

NY UNIT

First Assistant Cameras..........................NATE SPENGLER
....RACHEL BATASHVILI
Electrics..PHIL SOLOKOFF
....KATSUMI FUNAHASHI
Grips..MATT KEYSER
....CHARLIE MCGLINSKY
....ANGELIQUE STORER
Art Director...CAT NAVARRO
Leadman...ANDREW KECK
Art PA..NICK D'AMICO
Makeup.....................................MAGDALENA BUCZKOWSKA
Set Costumer.....................................HEATHER CAREY
Production Sound Mixer......................VIKTOR WEISZHAUPT
Production Assistants..................OLIVER SILVERTON-PEEL
....DREW PEDERSEN
Extras Casting..................................CENTRAL CASTING
Extras Casting Associate..........................BRAD KENNY

LA UNIT

First Assistant Camera............................ERIN NAIFEH
Key Grip..SARGON SAADI
Electric...ARIQ HANNAN
Makeup...ELIZABETH MBOUSIA
Hair...TINA FABULIC
Set Costumer....................................MELYNDA CHOOTHESA
Leadman..NICK BONNANO
Production Sound Mixer...............................JACK SOBO

POST PRODUCTION

Post Production Supervisor....................JEFFREY PENMAN
Assistant Editor..SAM LEVY
Post Production Accounting.................RACHEL SCHNEIDER,
....TREVANNA POST INC.
Post Production Assistant..........................TARA BAYAT
Supervising Sound Editor / Re-Recording Mixer.LEWIS GOLDSTEIN
ADR Editor / Re-Recording Mixer..................THOMAS RYAN
Dialogue Editor..................................ALFRED DEGRAND
Sound Effects Editor..................................ALEX SOTO
Foley Editor...................................WEN-HSUAN TSENG
Foley Artist.....................................SHAUN BRENNAN
Assistant Sound Editor.........................ALFRED DEGRAND
Assistant Sound Effects Editor.................LINZY ELLIOT
Audio Post Production Manager...................CATE MONTANA
Sound by...PARABOLIC
Additional ADR Provided by....................SOUNDLOUNGE-NY
Audio Studio Producer.............................ROB BROWNING
ADR Mixer...................................PATRICK CHRISTENSEN
ADR Voice Casting................DANN FINK AND BRUCE WINANT
Additional Voices......................................DANN FINK
....MARCELLA LENTZ POPE
....REBECCA SOLER
....BRUCE NIELSON WINANT
Supervising Digital Colorist..................ANDREW FRANCIS
Digital Intermediate Producer................ADAM SONNENFELD
Digital Intermediate Conform Editor...........PATRICK DEVINE
Digital Intermediate Color Assist............CHARLES LEIGHTON
Digital Intermediate Provided by..................SIXTEEN19

NY Dailies Provided by................HARBOR PICTURE COMPANY
NY Dailies Producer..............................MATT HAWKINS
NY Dailies Technician..............................ALEC PEREZ
....ERIK CHOQUETTE
Editorial Services Provided by........HARBOR PICTURE COMPANY
Editorial Producer...............................CARA MANISE
Support Engineers...............................GUATAM SINHA
....ALEX PATTISON
Title Design....................................TEDDY BLANKS
Stock Footage Coordinator..........................MIKE DAVIS
End Titles Created with...............................ENDCRAWL
Visual Effects by........................BRAINSTORM DIGITAL
Visual Effects Supervisor..........................ERAN DINUR
Visual Effects Producers...........................GLEN ALLEN
....RICHARD FRIEDLANDER
Composting Supervisor..............................MANI TRUMP
Lead Compositor....................................YUNSIK NOH
Digital Compositors.................................MINA CHOE
....CELESTE LEIZER
....UNGGYU CHOI
....JASMINE CARRUTHERS
....NAMJIN HEO
....JOSHUA BOLIVER
Digital Compositors.................................MINA CHOE
....CELESTE LEIZER
....UNGGYU CHOI
....JASMINE CARRUTHERS
....NAMJIN HEO
....JOSHUA BOLIVER
Lead Matte Painter............................NICK CONSTANDY
Matte Painters................................BEN ZYLBERMAN
....JIHYE KIM
CG Artist....................................ELANA LEDERMAN
Additional Visual Effects by........................KILL9 FX
Visual Effects Producer..........................JASON GANDHI
Visual Effects Artists.............................DAVE LEVINE
....BRIAN NUGENT
Additional Visual Effects by..............MECHANISM DIGITAL
Visual Effects Supervisor.....................LUCIEN HARRIOT
Visual Effects Executive Producer.............CHRIS PETERSON
Designer & Digital Compositor.....................FANGGE CHEN
Digital Compositor..........................CONSTANCE CONRAD
CGI Artist...................................MARK PALKOSKI
Additional Visual Effects by.........................4TH WALL
Visual Effects Executive Producer.....JAROM SALVATORE SIDWELL
Digital Team................................RYAN SONDEREGGER
....TYSON BENARD
....EVAN ROBERTS
....DAVID BURNHAM
....JOSHUA WILSON
Payroll Services Provided by.......................CAST & CREW
...........................ENTERTAINMENT SERVICES, LLC.
Production Counsel.........................COHEN GARDNER LLP
Production Attorney............................CARISSA KNOL
Production Consultant...........................DAMA CLAIRE
Camera Equipment Provided by......................PANAVISION
Camera and Electric Equipment Provided by.............MOVING
....PICTURES LTD.
Grip and Electric Equipment Provided by........REDMAN MOVIES
....AND STORIES
Camera Cart Equipment Provided by.....................NEBTEK
Sound Equipment Provided by......................TREW AUDIO
Hair and Makeup Provided by..........NIGEL'S BEAUTY EMPORIUM

STOCK FOOTAGE AND STILLS COURTESY OF

Pond5, Inc.
Shutterstock, Inc.

USED BY PERMISSION.

"Route One" Courtesy of the United States Department of Health, Education, and Welfare

"Teenager From Outerspace" Courtesy of Tom Graeff

ACKNOWLEDGMENTS

Batteries Plus Bulbs • Fire Station 6 • Freightsaver
Grand America • Hyatt Centric • Hyatt House
ISS / Studio Graphics • LDS Hospital • Marshall Moore
Movie Site Power And Lite • Park City Hospital
Salt Lake City Corporation • Salt Lake County Permits
Salt Lake City Police • Utah Highway Patrol
Utah Film Studios • Shuttlefreight, Ontario, CA
Silverado Lodge • Unified Police Department

SONGS

THE DARK SIDE OF THE SUN
Written by Gernot Bronsert
Performed by Modeselektor
Courtesy of Monkeytown
By arrangement with Friendly Fire Licensing

SLEDGE HAMMER (FEAT. B.O.B, HAVI, ROXXANNE, LONDON JAE & JAQUE BEATZ)
Written by Georg Philipp Telemann
Performed by B.o.B
Courtesy of Cherry Red
By arrangement with Friendly Fire Licensing

12 FANTAISIES: NO.6 IN D MINOR, TWV 40:7: DOLCE - ALLEGRO - SPIRITUOSO
Written by Georg Philipp Telemann
Performed by Benedek Csalog
Courtesy of Naxos of America, Inc.

VC COMMANDER
Written by Dustin Musser and Dylan Lewman
Performed by K Theory
Courtesy of Audiosocket

N*GGAS IN THE NIGHT (FEAT. THRILLAH)
Written by Jacob Cameron Smith & Daniel Kane
Performed by Cam Smith
Courtesy of Jacob Cameron Smith
By arrangement with Friendly Fire Licensing

BOTH SIDES NOW
Written by Joni Mitchell
Performed by Judy Collins
Courtesy of Elektra / Asylum Records
By arrangements with Warner Music Group Film & TV Licensing

THE FUN SONG
Performed by Flatbush Zombies
Courtesy of Glorius Dead Recordings

FILMED ON LOCATION IN UTAH
WITH SPECIAL THANKS TO THE STATE OF UTAH GOVERNOR'S OFFICE OF ECONOMIC DEVELOPMENT AND THE UTAH FILM COMMISSION

THIS PRODUCTION PARTICIPATED IN THE NEW YORK STATE
GOVERNOR'S OFFICE OF MOTION PICTURE & TELEVISION DEVELOPMENT'S
POST PRODUCTION CREDIT PROGRAM

SAG-AFTRA

SIXTEEN19

FILMED WITH PANAVISION CAMERAS,
LENSES, AND GRIP EQUIPMENT

HARBOR PICTURE COMPANY

51363 MOTION PICTURE ASSOCIATION OF AMERICA

PARABOLIC

HEREDITARY
By Ari Aster

A24 Films LLC
New York, NY
a24films.com

CREATIVE DIRECTION
Zoe Beyer

HEAD OF PUBLISHING
Perrin Drumm

PUBLISHING OPERATIONS MANAGER
Shayan Saalabi

EDITOR
Mark Lotto

COPY EDITOR
Nathan Stobaugh

COLORIST
Dave Herr

ART DIRECTION AND DESIGN
Actual Source
actualsource.work

TYPOGRAPHY
Isar Text Light
Isar Text Regular
Basel Grotesk
By Chi-Long Trieu

TIP-IN
Sticker Garda Gloss 135 gsm

PAPER
Munken Polar Rough 100 gsm
Garda Gloss 150 gsm

PRINTER
Conti Tipocolor

Fourth Printing, 2025

The publisher apologizes for any errors. Please send any corrections for future reprints or editions of this book to publishing@a24films.com.

ISBN 978-1-7339920-3-9

A24